The Eternal You

CARROLL E. SIMCOX

The Eternal You

*An Exploration of
a Spiritual Intuition*

CROSSROAD • NEW YORK

1986
The Crossroad Publishing Company
370 Lexington Avenue, New York, N.Y. 10017

Printed in the United States of America

Library of Congress Cataloging in Publication Data

Simcox, Carroll Eugene, 1912-
  The eternal you.

  1. Eternity.   2. Spiritual life—Anglican authors. I. Title.
BT912.S55   1986   236'.21   85-26981
ISBN 0-8245-0745-2

ACKNOWLEDGMENTS

Grateful acknowledgment for permission to quote copyrighted material in this book is made to the following publishers and agents:
    Burns & Oates Ltd., for the use of the full text of Alice Meynell's poem "Christ in the Universe";
    Concordia Publishing House, for the passage from Walter Künneth's book *The Theology of the Resurrection*;
    Dodd, Mead & Company, Inc., for the passage from G. K. Chesterton's *Orthodoxy*;
    Doubleday and Company, Inc., for the use of Rudyard's Kipling's poem "When Earth's Last Picture is Painted";
    Harvard University Press, for the passage from *Collected Papers of Charles Sanders Peirce*;
    Holt, Rinehart and Winston, for the use of two lines from Robert Frost's poem *Birches*;
    A. P. Watt Ltd., Literary Agents, for the use of one stanza from G. K. Chesterton's poem "The House of Christmas."

This book is a thank offering for, and to, those "wonderful Dead who have passed through the body and gone" (Browning), who by their living and dying have taught me that "there is a land of the living and a land of the dead and the bridge is love, the only survival, the only meaning" (Wilder).

C.E.S.

CONTENTS

PROLOGUE

Let us think much of rest—the rest which is not of indolence, but of powers in perfect equilibrium. The rest which is as deep as summer midnight, yet full of life and force as summer sunshine, the Sabbath of eternity. Let us think of the love of God, which we shall feel in full tide upon our souls. Let us think of that marvelous career of sublime occupation which shall belong to the spirits of just men made perfect; when we shall fill a higher place in God's universe, and more consciously, and with more distinct oversight, cooperate with God in the rule over his creation.

Frederick W. Robertson

Heaven is under our feet as well as over our heads.

Henry David Thoreau

The world is peopled only to people heaven.

St. Francis de Sales

Entrance into heaven is not at the hour of death, but at the moment of conversion.

Benjamin Whichcote

ONE

A PASSIONATE INTUITION

One in whom persuasion and belief
Has ripened into faith, and faith become
A passionate intuition.
William Wordsworth, "An Excursion"

"Every man is his own doctor of divinity, in the last resort."[1] Emboldened by these words of Stevenson I am undertaking to set forth a strong conviction, a passionate intuition, about the Things Unseen that are eternal. I seem to hear one of my revered mentors, Doctor Johnson, warning me against such audacity. When he was told about a mystical enthusiast who claimed a vision of things unutterable he remarked that if they were indeed unutterable the man would be well advised not to try to utter them. *Touché*. But I am not claiming a vision, only a conviction. It is, however, strong enough to claim me as well as to be claimed by me.

A conviction, not an opinion. It has been said that many people know their opinions, few their convictions, but that in the long run their convictions determine their destinies while their opinions merely flutter and fade. Opinions are intellectual beliefs, and in good minds they are always held tentatively, subject to instant revision. They usually change, and when they do we can always hope that it is for the better. An opinion is confined to the mind, and most opinions seem to have little effect upon the conduct of those who hold them.

A conviction is more complex and usually more influential. Where a conviction and an opinion collide in one person the conviction always prevails, if it is strong enough to be a conviction.

Our convictions rule us for better or for worse, and not necessarily for better. The bigot, the fanatic, the persecutor is always driven by a passionate conviction of the rightness of his cause, but then so is the saint and so is the heavy contributor of any lasting good to the world's treasury.

The theme with variations of this book is a conviction, a passionate intuition, which may be simply stated: *You, I, all human beings, indeed all things animate and inanimate, visible and invisible, are eternal.* You existed in the mind of God—therefore you existed before time and the world began. You exist in God now, you will exist in him forever, as will every*body* and every*thing*. A million years ago you existed and were being created prenatally. You were not yet incarnate and you had no self-awareness, but God was creating you and knowing exactly what he was doing. He is creating you now, knowing exactly what he is doing, and making no mistakes, whatever you may think or fear. He will be creating you a million years from now in a dimension of being in which time is not measured by years and space is not measured by miles.

I am far more certain of the truth of this conviction than I am of any opinion I hold, but here we need to note an important similarity between a conviction and an opinion. If both the conviction and the opinion inhabit the same good mind they are both held subject to revision, amendment, or abandonment if at any time experience or evidence demands it. My conviction has held me for a long time, but it has changed and developed up to now and it would be absurd for me to claim finality for the whole of it or for any part of it.

Moreover, my conviction is in the *truth*-category rather than the *fact*-category, and this distinction must be clearly observed. Whatever I assert on the basis of my conviction may or may not be *true*, but it must be *incorrect*. There can be correctness only in strictly factual statements that are flawlessly accurate on all points of pertinent fact. A fact, as distinct from a truth, is a *factum*, a thing settled and done (so far as we can see), an incontestable obviosity such as that today is the day between yesterday and tomorrow.

A correct statement is a complete one; it says all that can presently be said about the subject. For example: "According to all the evidence we have, the Battle of Hastings took place in 1066." This statement is subject to correction only if fresh evidence one day shows that the date or the place referred to is wrong. Until then, it is a correct statement. My conviction is now and forever infinitely correctable because it is a truth-statement rather than a fact-statement. We can know "the facts of the case" but never "the truth of the matter" until we know the *whole* story—and that is never possible in this life. When in court we swear to tell the whole truth we know not what we say and the law knows not what it asks. Therefore, I may assert as a conviction what I profoundly believe to be the truth about our being. I may not assert it as a fact any more than its gainsayer may assert its falsehood.

At our birth we enter the realm of fact from the realm of truth, without losing our citizenship in the latter.[2] At death we reenter the realm of truth, with something significantly added. Of this, more later.

When St. Paul spoke of the things temporal and the things eternal, by the former he meant facts, by the latter he meant truth.[3] Facts belong only to space-time, yet beyond time they have their eternal rootage in those truths of which, in the here and now, they are fractional incarnations. You and I are facts: fractional incarnations of our eternal selves. We say of a well-established fact that it is true as far as it goes, that is, to the extent that it expresses the truth which it incarnates. You and I are true "as far as we go" in our present existence. Our destiny is to become by God's grace our wholly true selves by being completed; and before we can thus come true, become complete, we must experience our present facthood.

We can think and speak of truth, the Things Unseen, symbolically, and only so. "We are symbols, and we inhabit symbols," as Emerson says.[4]

A true symbol both reflects and conveys an authentic part of the truth it symbolizes. No symbol can express its whole truth. A "time beyond time" will come when we shall be able to say, as Jesus did, that no longer must we speak in "proverbs" (symbolic speech) but we shall show one another "plainly of the Father."[5]

What I have been saying will largely explain why I lean so heavily upon poets in my rationale. Santayana said somewhere, "Our religion is the poetry in which we believe."[6] He meant one thing by that statement and I mean another as I make it my own. In my view, the truths of God and his purposes for creation are such that they can only be symbolically apprehended and expressed in our present mode of being; hence they are "the poetry in which we believe." Santayana believed that this "poetry" is fictional rather than representational.

God only knows what Disraeli had in mind when he made this astounding remark: "The Athanasian Creed is the most splendid ecclesiastical lyric ever poured forth by the genius of man."[7] I cannot give that strange dogmatic composition nearly so high a rating as lyric poetry. But it is a poem, a symbol. It is noteworthy that "symbol" is one of the earliest Christian synonyms for "creed." From the beginning, the teachers, preachers, and professors of Christianity have recognized that all truth-statements about God and his works and ways are necessarily symbolic.

I quote such authorities as Emily Brontë and Wordsworth and Meynell and Chesterton more than I quote Kant and Bultmann and Barth and Tillich because, for me, they are more validly authoritative. A poet or mystic "sees" a truth by feeling it, yet not merely by feeling it. If he is intelligent, as all good poets and mystics are, he unceasingly inspects his feelings with his mind and conscience. His feelings are intuitions, passionate and yet rational and moral. He trusts them as guides to truth, and still more as messengers *of* truth *from* Truth. The conventional philosopher or theologian does not trust his feelings in any such way. Such vision as the poet or mystic claims is hardly his cup of tea; for him "visionary" is a suspect word. He eschews poetry or any other form of deliberately symbolic language as a proper idiom for communication, although, of course, he is forced to use symbolism in spite of his distrust of it because nobody, not even he, can say much of anything except symbolically.

"Metaphysics is the finding of bad reasons for what we believe upon instinct," said F. M. Bradley.[8] Perhaps he was too hard on the metaphysicians, of whom he himself was one. We might emend his aphorism to read: "Metaphysics is the finding of inadequate reasons for what we believe by intuition." Good theology is the finding of inadequate reasons for what we already believe about God, truth, and ourselves by that intuition which is born of faith and love. Bad theology is — everything else.

I am about to quote a passage from Chesterton, partly for the pleasure of running through it again but mainly because in its last three sentences is wittily and rightly expressed the reason for my preference in the matter of authority. It reads:

> Imagination does not breed insanity. Exactly what does breed insanity is reason. Poets do not go mad; but chessplayers do. Mathematicians go mad, and cashiers; but creative artists very seldom. . . . Perhaps the strongest case of all is this: that only one great English poet went mad, Cowper. And he was definitely driven mad by logic, by the ugly and alien logic of predestination. Poetry was not the disease, but the medicine; poetry kept him partly in health. . . . He was damned by John Calvin; he was almost saved by John Gilpin.[9] . . . Poetry is sane because it floats so easily on an infinite sea; reason seeks to cross the infinite sea, and so make it finite. The result is mental exhaustion, like the physical exhaustion of Mr. Holbein. To accept everything is an exercise, to understand everything is a strain. The poet only desires exaltation and expansion, a world to stretch himself in. The poet only asks to get his head into the heavens. It is the logician who seeks to get the heavens into his head. And it is the head that splits.[10]

It was sometime in the 1930s when I first read that passage. Through it, and through some other inspired words of the wise, the Holy Spirit has taught me how to read a poem, listen to a song, view a picture. I am to sit down in front of it, open my eyes, ears, mind, and heart, and shut my mouth; to look, listen, open, and receive. The poem or song or picture has something it wants to give me if I will be so good to it and to myself as to let it do so. But that is not the ultimately right way of putting the matter. It is God, speaking through the poet, who would speak to me through the poem. The poem can convey God's word to me (every truth is God speaking) if I will let it come to me, if I don't rush out to meet it in order to tell it all about myself and perhaps all about itself, as does the bad poet and bad listener in this doggerel:

> *Twinkle, twinkle, little star.*
> *I don't wonder what you are.*
> *What you are I know quite well,*
> *And your component parts can tell.*

The poet sanely lets himself float on the infinite sea instead of trying to conquer it by crossing it. Thus he can listen to the music of the spheres, and if he is any kind of a poet he can pass on to us something of what he hears. What we shall get, if the circuit is completed, is a vision of some truth, though not a total inventory of the truth with precisely itemized descriptions of everything in it.

Expansion, a world in which to stretch himself, is what the poet wants. And it is precisely what I want, what I am sure God wants all of us to have.

Chesterton mentions the one English poet who went mad, William Cowper: damned by John Calvin, almost saved by John Gilpin. He who wrote the rollicking "*Diverting History of John Gilpin*" wrote also "*Light Shining out of Darkness,*"[11] in which appears this glorious stanza:

Deep in unfathomable mines
Of never failing skill
He treasures up his bright designs,
And works his sovereign will.

Every one of those adjectives has revelatory impact: "unfathomable"—beyond our comprehension; "never failing"—omnicompetent; "bright"—radiantly beautiful as God's designs truly are when seen as only God can perfectly see them; sovereign—alone having power, invincible, sure, certain. How could a merely prosaic mind see what Cowper sees? How could a merely factual pen ever communicate his vision?

I wholeheartedly subscribe to the catholic creeds of Christendom, the Apostles' and the Nicene; but in my expanding self I go well beyond the bounds of official orthodoxy. And why not? To go beyond the creed is not to deny or contradict it but to use it as a launching pad. Some among my orthodox friends frown upon such goings beyond "the faith once delivered"[12] as this is articulated in the creeds. I consider this restrictive and exclusionary principle wrong. Christian thinking properly begins with the creed rather than ending with it. Christ tells us that the Spirit will lead us *into* all truth.[13] The Greek word translated "lead" is related to the word for "road." The promise is that he will lead us not simply *to* truth but *into* it. There is always more truth ahead of us on this journey through time, and I cannot doubt that Christ our guide will lead us eternally on this journey into truth. Hence the creed, being the Gospel in summary, is properly the starting mark and not the finish line for the journey of faith.

Much of what I affirm in what follows you may take or leave without thereby making yourself a better Christian or a worse one. This is simply a passionate intuition that enables at least one Christian believer to expand and stretch himself infinitely, to his soul's delight.

NOTES

1. Robert Louis Stevenson, *An Inward Voyage.*
2. "Our citizenship is in heaven" (Philippians 3:20).
3. 2 Corinthians 4:18.
4. Ralph Waldo Emerson, *Essays, First Series,* "The Poet."
5. John 16:25.
6. I cannot find this among Santayana's published works, but I have no doubt that he said it.
7. In a speech at the Guildhall, London, 9 November 1878.
8. F. H. Bradley, *Appearance and Reality* (1893).
9. Very few people I know seem to have read this hilariously funny poem by Cowper. We had it in our sixth-grade reader back in the age when good King Calvin reigned in the land and snoozed in the White House. Whatever has become of good literature in our schools?
10. G. K. Chesterton, *Orthodoxy* (New York: Dodd, Mead, 1937), p. 28.
11. William Cowper, *Olney Hymns*, XXXV, bk. iii, 15.
12. Jude 3.
13. John 16:13.

TWO

MUSEMENT

By intuition, mightiest things
Assert themselves, and not by terms.
"I'm midnight!"—need the midnight say?
"I'm sunrise!—need the Majesty?
                                    Emily Dickinson

I am indebted to the American philosopher Charles Sanders Peirce (1839–1914) for the lovely word that provides title and theme for this chapter. Musement must not be confused with amusement. It doesn't mean anything like doing something just for kicks, or to kill time. When I use the word I mean exactly what he means by it, as set forth in this paragraph:

> There is a certain agreeable occupation of mind which, from its having no distinctive name, I infer is not as commonly practiced as it deserves to be; for indulged in moderately—some five or six per cent of one's waking time, perhaps during a stroll—it is refreshing enough more than to repay the expenditure. Because it involves no purpose save that of casting aside all serious purpose, I have sometimes been half inclined to call it reverie with some qualification; but for a frame of mind so antipodal to vacancy and dreaminess such a designation would be too excru-

ciating a misfit. In fact, it is Pure Play. Now, Play, as we all know, is a lively exercise of one's powers. Pure Play has no rules, except this very law of liberty: It bloweth where it listeth. It has no purpose, unless recreation.[1]

Musement and intuition are Siamese twins of the mind, quite inseparable. Musement is a way of thinking—playful yet serious; and intuition frequently, if not always, results from it.

Intuition (from *intueri*) is not seeing things but seeing *into* things. Alexis Carrel said of it: "Intuition comes very close to clairvoyance; it appears to be the extrasensory perception of reality."[2] He was speaking scientifically rather than philosophically, and I'm sure that very many of his sober-minded scientific colleagues would demur at such words as "clairvoyance" and "extrasensory perception of reality." Even so, many scientific discoverers testify that their revolutionary findings resulted from strange intuitions or hunches that came to them in moments when they were engaging in what we are calling musement. Young Isaac Newton in his twenty-fifth year watched an apple fall, mused upon it, mentally exclaimed in wonder something like "Aha! What have we here?" What he was given to see in that musement was the law of universal gravitation.

Peirce reminds us that musement, pure play of the mind, is a lively exercise of one's powers. There is pleasure in it, but it is stimulating pleasure, not narcotic. When the true muser is about it, his play is not like that of a bored little boy walking along kicking a can because there's nothing else to do. It involves a lively use of one's powers, yet not grimly so, like that of the bridge-player who "plays for blood."

Such playful thinking often proves to be the most productive and fruitful thinking about any subject under the sun—or over it. When you examine the etymology of the word "play" in any good dictionary you find that in the primary sense of the word there is in it more of the element of freedom, like that of a soaring and wide-ranging eagle, than of just fun-and-games. When, for example, the author of Psalm 8 let his mind muse playfully (*stricto sensu*) upon the moon and the stars which God had ordained, he was given to see, as by revelation, that God had made man but little lower than the angels to crown him with glory. It seems to be ever thus. We muse upon something for the sheer pleasure of musing upon it, and God gives us a pleasant surprise in the form of a vision or a sense of something we had not had before.

And now for a wild surmise. May it just be that this pure play of the mind provides an opening for the most high and playful God to reveal to the muser some wonderful truth? I do not hesitate to call God playful if we may trust whatever scriptural testimonies on the subject speak to the point either expressly or by implication. "Thou art worthy, O Lord, to receive glory and honor and power: for thou hast created all things, and for thy pleasure they are and were created."[3] "God saw every thing that he had made, and, behold, it was very good."[4] Jesus proclaims and reveals to us a Father who delights in his children. To be sure, God's musing upon his own works and creatures is not playful in the way that ours is, with the venturesomeness of wonder and childlike curiosity, but it is playful with the eye and mind and heart and will of perfect love. A mother musing upon her newborn first child is like God in her musing: Her mind plays lovingly upon what she has wrought.

Our musement of awe and wonder is our response (perhaps unconscious on our part) to his musement of fathering love. That great astronomer and deeply godly man, Johann Kepler, used to exclaim rapturously "O God, I think thy thoughts after thee!" His mind-play was in direct response to God's mind-play.

William Blake had a marvelously playful mind; so much so that many people whose minds played little or not at all thought him crazy. He told us that when he saw the sun rising he did not see a round disc of fire somewhat like a guinea, but rather "an innumerable company of the heavenly host crying, 'Holy, Holy, Holy, is the Lord God Almighty!' "[5] There's no doubt in my mind that he saw that scene in heaven, which is the heart and power-center of all reality, because the most playful God showed it to him. God delights in the vision of whatever he has made, and he wants us to join him in the enjoyment of it all. The one and only prerequisite to such enjoyment by mortals is a mind given to loving musement. Martin Buber taught us that God created man to be his partner in the dialogue of time. Alfred North Whitehead taught us that God wants his human creature to rise to a companioning relationship with him. His famous aphorism will always bear repeating: "Religion is what the individual does with his own solitariness. It runs through three stages, if it evolves to its final satisfaction. It is the transition from God the void to God the enemy, and from God the enemy to God the companion."[6] What is a companion, in the highest and deepest and ultimate sense of that word, if he is not somebody who walks with you and looks at the same things you look at and shares the whole of life with you and laughs and cries with you and virtually lives and dies with you? God wants his human creature to be his companion in that total sense. And at the present temporal stage of our companionship with him the medium of our dialogical discourse, our conversation, is our musement upon "the glories of his righteousness, and wonders of his love."[7]

Musement has no rules except this one perfect law of liberty: It bloweth where it listeth. When Peirce wrote that, he was quoting some words of Jesus to Nicodemus (John 3:18) as reported in the King James Version of the Bible. Jesus said that the Spirit of God in man is like a wind that simply goes wherever it feels inclined to go. A modern meteorologist might say that a wind is not really autonomous and self-directing at all; but if he said it aloud he would convict himself of lacking the capacity for musement. The Holy Spirit is like a wind that knows exactly where it is going (or would, of it were a rational wind), whereas the tiny pollen flake it carries along knows nothing of whence it comes and whither it goes. A human being has the wonderful and perilous power to choose whether or not to give himself over in trusting surrender to the wind of the Spirit, as did Abraham coming out from his safe and snug home in Ur, not knowing whither he went. Dr. George Washington Carver is best known and remembered as a scientific researcher into the nutritional and industrial uses of the peanut. But he became what he was by being a muser resonating to the musement of God. It is remembered that he began each day's work in his laboratory by sitting down in front of a peanut and asking God to show him something about the peanut that he didn't yet know. That of course was a kind of directed musing. (Isn't all authentic prayer a kind of longing musement directed toward God?)

I well remember a musement of my own that took place many years ago as I was lying in a hammock slung between two trees. I was daydreaming, woolgathering, as I looked up at the clouds. The air was quite still at ground level, but evidently more active at cloud level, so the clouds were distinctly moving and combining and recombining in myriad formations, assuming definite but transient shapes and forms. My mind began (unbidden by my will) to reflect upon the mystery that at each of these successive moments the molecules that made up those clouds, and indeed those of the whole universe, were in a "picture" that would never again be seen, exactly as it was, by God, angel, or man. Shelley's line came to me: "Nought may endure but Mutability."[8]

It was by no means an unwelcome or melancholy reflection, at least at the outset. I thought, how nice, how beautiful it is, that some things that happen to us can happen only once, then are gone forever as was this particular cloud formation at this particular moment. In short, nothing continues to exist for a moment beyond its actual occurrence. Sometimes that fact may call for tears, other times for *Te Deums*, but fact it is. The only thing that lasts for a thousand years or for a split second is change itself. In five minutes I shall not be able to see the sky-picture of this present moment because it will have passed into oblivion; but correction: I can't see it even now, because it's gone. What I called "this present moment" in ten seconds is no longer present. In fact, it never was, because there never is a present moment. What we call a present moment is the past becoming the future.

I shall never see that sky again just as it was a minute ago: at least not in time. But it has not passed into oblivion with God, for whom there is no oblivion. It is now eternal—a part of the world that is incessantly becoming because God is incessantly creating it. So what shall we say? Is that sky-picture gone forever, or is it "here" forever? What we are now calling "here" is by no means confined to this hammock on which I am lying, between these two trees, behind this summer home of my friend where I am on vacation. "Here" is the whole world as God sees it *sub specie aeternitatis*, that is, as it completely and forever really is.

This musement that began as I lay in the hammock cloudgazing about thirty years ago simply continued. I have a feeling, though I can't prove its validity and have no wish to argue it, that once God starts a musement in a human mind he keeps it going, even though he may let it run like an underground stream through the subconscious, intermittently rising to our consciousness. It is one way he has of educating us for an ever-increasing knowledge and love of him, and communion and fellowship with him. For what is communion and fellowship with God, or with anybody else, if it is not what we commonly call a meeting of minds? A meeting of minds is an intermeshing of two separate thought-processes.

If I am right about what I was given to see that day in my musement, what God showed me then and is continuing to show me all along must be true of he is not a deceiver and I am not deceived. Antoine de Saint-Exupéry in his musement was led to say: "Life has taught us that love does not consist in gazing at each other but in looking outward in the same direction."[9] That is not a total definition of love, and was not intended to be, but it is an acute perception of one primary characteristic of love. We all know that the more closely we share with somebody any kind of looking in the same direction, seeing some thing or things together with a common interest and concern—whatever that interest may be—the closer together in unitive love grow our minds, hearts, and lives. My conclusion and final conviction is that the divine Muser gives us the capacity and inclination for musement in the hope that he and we may grow together into a constant "looking in the same direction." In my passionate intuition this is the beginning and foretaste of glory—the eternal sharing of a vision and enjoyment of things as they eternally are.

NOTES

1. Charles Sanders Peirce, *The Collected Papers of Charles Sanders Peirce*, ed. Charles Hartshorne and Paul Weiss (Cambridge, Mass.: Harvard University Press, 1935), vol. VI. Quoted from Hartshorne and Reese, *Philosophers Speak of God* (Chicago: University of Chicago Press, 1953), p. 259.
2. Alexis Carrel, *Reflections on Life*. Quoted from *The Crown Treasury of Relevent Quotations*, ed. E. F. Murphy (New York: Crown Publishers, Inc., 1978), p. 382.
3. Revelation 4:11.
4. Genesis 1:31.
5. William Blake, "A Vision of the Last Judgment."
6. Alfred North Whitehead, *Religion in the Making* (New York: The Macmillan Company, 1926), p. 16.
7. From the hymn "Joy to the World," by Isaac Watts (1719).
8. Percy Bysshe Shelley, "Mutability."
9. Antoine de Saint-Exupéry, *Wind Sand, and Stars*, trans. Lewis Galantière (New York: Harcourt, Brace, & World, 1939). Quoted from *The International Thesaurus of Quotations*, ed. Rhonda Thomas Tripp (New York: Thomas Y. Crowell Company, Inc., 1970), p. 372.

THREE

THE PLEASING,
DREADFUL THOUGHT

Eternity! thou pleasing, dreadful thought!
Joseph Addison, *Cato*

Sir Thomas Browne asked, "Who can speak of eternity without a solecism, or think thereof without an ecstasy?"[1] The first part of his question may be answered: Nobody. The second part must be answered: Many times too many.

If we try to speak of eternity in our language of space-time-flesh we can only speak incorrectly, for the reason we noted in the first chapter in the distinction between truth and fact. This is no reason, however, why we should not think and speak of it as best we can.

If we meditate upon eternity as our native land, from which we are temporarily absent, we may feel either homesickness, or joy, or both: homesickness because "the night is dark, and I am far from home,"[2] joy in the prospect of a homegoing that will be a home-coming.

Browne said also: "The created world is but a small parenthesis in eternity."[3] He was expressing the conventional view of eternity as simply an inconceivably long time, as in this passage in the New Testament: "One day is with the Lord as a thousand years, and thousand years as one day."[4] That is to identify eternity with everlastingness. To be sure, everlastingness is a dimension of eternity, but it is by no means the quiddity of it

Eternity is *being in God*. Whatever is in God is eternal. This is not to say that whatever is *in* God is *of* God, a part or flake of God, or an emanation of God's own substance. The Moslems are at great pains to declare "There is no God but God!" Christians must be equally emphatic on the point and keep the distinction between Creator and creature categorically absolute.

In the New Testament writings bearing the name of John we are taught to think of eternal life as life in God. "God is love; he that dwelleth in love dwelleth in God, and God in him."[5] When Browne said that the created world is but a parenthesis in eternity he spoke more truthfully than he knew, but in a different sense from what he intended. Life in this world is life in eternity, albeit parenthetical life. A parenthesis within a sentence is a part of the sentence. When we awaken to love, in the New Testament sense of the word,[6] we awaken to awareness of who we eternally are, and of "where" we eternally are—in God: here and now only parenthetically, no doubt, but truly and completely. Whenever we love as Christ loves we experience our eternal selfhood. Well says Thoreau: "Being is the great explainer."[7] The only explanation of our eternal being in God that we get in this present life is given to us by being itself—as an awareness. Blake says somewhere that "every act of love is a little death in the divine image." It is a dying into the life of God, a self-authenticating expression of eternal life: "We know that we have passed from death to life, because we love the brethren."[8]

Blaise Pascal was a devout Christian but hardly a jubilant one. In his *Pensées* we read: "When I consider the short duration of my life, swallowed up in the eternity before and after, the little space which I fill, or even can see, engulfed in the infinite immensity of spaces of which I am ignorant, and which know me not, I am frightened, and am astonished at being here rather than there; for there is no reason why here rather than there, why now rather than then. Who has put me here? By whose order and direction have this place and time been allotted to me? *Memoria hospitis unius diei praetereuntis.*"[9]

That is sad talk. For Pascal, eternity is not a pleasing thought but a dreadful one. It gives him no joy in the midst of this frightful world. But the good tidings of great joy, the gospel of Jesus Christ, comes to us from eternity and is about eternity, about God "our eternal home."[10]

Consider by contrast the exuberance of Richard Jefferies, a nineteenth-century English naturalist: "It is eternity now. I am in the midst of it, as the butterfly in the light-laden air. Nothing has to come; it is now. Now is eternity; now is the immortal life."[11] If he believed that eternity is contained *by* our temporal now, rather than containing it, he was wrong; but evidently he did not. He had that loving and joyful *feel* of eternity which too many Christians unaccountably lack. I say "unaccountably" because Christians ought to get their idea of eternity from their idea of God, and get their idea of God from their vision of Christ.

When as a child I became acquainted with Isaac Watts's great hymn, "*O God, Our Help in Ages Past,*" I was struck by its reference to God as "our eternal home." Ever since, I have felt that there is some danger of misconception in thinking of heaven as a sort of place, or even ambience, in which God dwells but which is external to himself as my house is external to me. When eventually I learned that the hymn is a paraphrase of Psalm 90 and that the phrase "our eternal home" faithfully echoes the opening verse of that Psalm, I realized that this is how the Hebrew poet experienced God— as his home. God is more than our home, but he is our home. He has been our home "in all generations"[12] and will be our home forever. And he is not only *our* home, but the home of all that he has made; and he has made and is making all that exists, including those things we commonly consider creations of our own. To create (as distinct from to construct) is to make something our of nothing; whence it follows that only God can create.

An example of that is Pioneer 10. On 14 June 1983 we read in our newspapers: "Pioneer 10 sped beyond Neptune's orbit for an eternal trip through the Milky Way galaxy Monday, becoming the first man-made object to leave the solar system and reach outer space.''[13] This story is a real mind boggler. Alan Fernquist, assistant flight director of NASA's Ames Research Center, was quoted as saying: ''The spacecraft will probably survive forever. It will not encounter any other objects. Over the next million years it will not come closer than three light years to any known stars. In that time, Pioneer's closest approach to a star probably will take place in 32,610 years when it passes within 3.3 light years from the red dwarf, Ross 248.''

You and I shall not be around in our present abode to see how it all comes out; but when we have returned Home we shall see it instantly—in the Eternal Now. How can I be so sure of that? Well, remember that it is an intuition, not a theorem. And because it is what it is, naturally I am surer of it than I could possibly be if some wizard of cosmic lore were to demonstrate the certainty of it to me.

We are only beginning to realize how vast this universe is, and the astronomers tell us that it is rapidly growing. Yet its physical vastness is but a symbol of the immensity of God. ''He's got the whole wide world in his hand.'' There are no light years to him— nor to those to whom he is Home. For him, and therefore for them, there are no past, present, and future, because all is present to him simultaneously.

''I do not believe in dwelling upon the distances which are supposed to dwarf the world,'' said Chesterton. ''I think there is even something a trifle vulgar about this idea of trying to rebuke spirit by size.''[14] Somebody, I think it was Gavarni, gave us this pertinent apothegm: ''Astronomically speaking, what is man? Astronomically speaking, man is the astronomer.''[15] Man is the astronomer because of the Word or Reason (*Logos*) of God in him. Man's mind is at once a symbol and an instrument of God's mind. God reasons in and through man (though not *only* through man). When a person is thinking soundly he generally has some sense that he's not doing this all by himself, but that somehow reality is thinking through him.

Fernquist thinks that the spacecraft will probably last forever. I have no doubt that it will last forever. God created it, through man, and so it exists. When Fernquist used the word "forever" he was thinking temporally, but "forever" is really a metaphysical term, neither physical nor temporal. It means world without end, and that means the world as it exists in God. Pioneer 10, like you and me, is a creature that existed in the mind of God before the worlds began; and, like you and me, it has an eternal destiny, a foreverness that is beyond time.

Yet so, no less, has the gnat whose mortal span is only a few hours.

> Time, like an ever-rolling stream,
> Bears all its sons away;
> They fly, forgotten, as a dream
> Dies at the opening day.[16]

Forgotten upon earth, yes. Forgotten in God, never.

The penitent thief on the cross said to Jesus, "Lord, remember me when you come into your kingdom." And Jesus replied, "You may be sure that today you will be with me in paradise."[17] The man may have been thinking only that he would love to live beyond death, especially in a kingdom ruled by this strange and beautiful man who was dying with him only a few feet away. But any human statement, spoken by anybody in any circumstances, always means more than is in the speaker's conscious mind, and so here. Dismas (let's call him that—everyone else does) deeply wanted God to be mindful of him, and he recognized God in Jesus. Unconsciously he knew that *to be in God's mind is to be.*

He was not a philosopher and so the words *Esse est percipi*, "to be is to be perceived," would have meant nothing to him. But their truth he intuitively knew. To be remembered by Jesus, to be seen by God, is to exist eternally. Had he been born in the right time and place Dismas might have enjoyed two limericks on this theme. Perhaps he is enjoying them now as he attends our discussion. The first is by some unknown craftsman of this demanding art form who was perplexed by the *esse est percipi* principle, and so he wrote:

> *There was a young man who said, "God*
> *Must think it exceedingly odd*
>   *That this sycamore tree*
>   *Continues to be*
> *When there's no one about in the quad."*

To this Monsignor Ronald A. Knox made this famous rejoinder:

> *Dear Sir: Your astonishment's odd.*
> *I am always about in the quad.*
>   *And that's why this tree*
>   *Will continue to be*
> *Since observed by—Yours faithfully, God.*

To be perceived by God is to exist. And if everything God ever created is perceived by him, if he never forgets or loses sight of anybody or anything, if he never scraps anybody or anything—I was going to say that you may draw your own conclusions. But how many options do you have? There is only one, really, that you can reasonably draw, and that is that nobody or nothing that God ever makes ever ceases to be.

NOTES

1. Sir Thomas Browne, *Religio Medici*.
2. John Henry Newman, *The Pillar of Cloud*, "Lead Kindly Light."
3. Browne, *Christian Morals*.
4. 2 Peter 3:8.
5. 1 John 4:16b.
6. *Agape* love, whose object is the good of the beloved rather than the self of the lover.
7. Henry David Thoreau, *Journal*, 26 February 1841.
8. 1 John 3:14.

9. Blaise Pascal, *Pensées,* 205, trans. W. F. Trotter (New York: Random House, 1941). The cryptic Latin may be translated, "A stranger's memory of one fleeting day."

10. Isaac Watts, "O God, Our Help in Ages Past," st. 1.

11. Richard Jefferies, *The Story of My Heart.*

12. Psalm 90:1.

13. Associated Press release, 14 June 1983.

14. G. K. Chesterton, *The Everlasting Man* (London: Hodder & Stoughton, 1925), p. 23.

15. "Gavarni" was the pseudonym of Sulpice Guillaume Chevalier (1804–1866).

16. Watts, *op. cit.,* st. 5.

17. Luke 23:42–43.

FOUR

GOD LOVING GOD

> God alone is capable of loving God. We can only
> consent to give up our own feelings so as to
> allow free passage in our soul for this love. That
> is the meaning of denying oneself. We are created
> for this consent, and for this alone.
> Simone Weil, *Waiting on God*

There is one question that any Christian teacher must be prepared to answer, especially if he conducts teaching missions as I have done over many years. The question is: How can I love God? It may go on to say: I know that I am commanded to love God, but I just can't do it in the way that I love my child or my spouse. And besides, I don't see how love can be commanded.

In earlier years I used to fumble badly over this one until I learned to give this simple answer: You can love God be getting out of his way and thus letting him love himself through you. Simone Weil is right: Only God can love God. But by realizing and actualizing our own being in him we become living channels of his love as he pours it forth in two directions: to himself, as God, and to all his creatures. He gives us the power to choose between being open channels and closed ones. The one thing that can close that channel

25

in us is the kind of self-love in which we imagine that we live outside of God. We do not and we cannot, but we can imagine that we do; and it may well be that living in that false imagination is the very essence of what we call hell.

"Two cities have been formed by two loves," wrote St. Augustine, "the earthly city by the love of self to the contempt of God, and the heavenly city by the love of God to the contempt of self."[1]

Indeed you cannot love God in the way that you love your child or parent or spouse or friend. They are your fellow creatures; they exist with you in God; you love them in God. Your love for God cannot be simply your love for your fellow creatures carried to the nth degree; it is in an entirely different order. It is adoration and self-offering: adoration for his goodness by which you live, self-offering as grateful response to his gift of all that you are and all that you have. As you give yourself to him, he makes you a channel through whom he pours forth his love upon all creatures whose lives you touch. All of this two-way operation takes place in him. The loving is all his; what you call your love for him is a reflection of his love; your love for your child or your enemy is his love working through you.

I have been asked more than once whether this divine love is to be thought of as God's or Christ's. The New Testament writers speak of this love interchangably as the love of God and the love of Christ, and that is correct. Like the Holy Spirit, this love proceeds from the Father and the Son; or, if you prefer, from the Father through the Son. It is the same love.

When St. Augustine speaks of those who love self to the contempt of God he is talking about people who in culpable folly, rebelling against their vocation to be obedient instruments of God's love, go off all on their own—in their warped imagination. In them egocentricity usurps the place of theocentricity. Morally and spiritually they live "without God in the world"[2] until they repent. Yet they *exist* in God, since he has created them, even as they *live* "without" him. I hope this does not strike you as intolerably hairsplitting.

Later I will present my case for considering this distinction as not only desirable but essential.

God is "not a God of the dead, but the God of the living: for all live unto him," said Jesus.[3] *All*; not just the godly. Here I am creating a theological problem for myself. What happens to the invincibly reprobate in the end? Hell, and all that? Patience; we'll get to "all that," I promise you; but first there are some bridges to cross.

One poem more than any other has influenced my mind in the direction it takes in this book: Emily Brontë's *Last Lines*. Here are the closing stanzas:

> *With wide-embracing love*
> *Thy spirit animates eternal years,*
> *   Pervades and broods above,*
> *Changes, sustains, dissolves, creates, and rears.*

> *   Though earth and man were gone,*
> *And suns and universes ceased to be,*
> *   And thou wert left alone,*
> *Every existence would exist in thee.*

> *   There is not room for Death,*
> *Nor atom that his might could render void:*
> *   Thou—thou art Being and Breath,*
> *And what thou art may never be destroyed.*

These lines convey to me God's answer to the painful contemporary question: What happens if somebody in Washington or Moscow pushes the button and the result is a world in which there are no buttons left to push and nobody left to push them? In answer to that we may recall a line in Father Knox's limerick: "I am always about in the quad." Equally true it is to say that the quad will be always about in God. The world as we presently know it can indeed be blasted to rubble. But this world is in God, and can it be destroyed "there" even by the superpowers with their superbombs?

Sydney Harris asks: "If we finally manage to explode the whole planet in atomic warfare, does anyone imagine that we will be blowing ourselves up to Kingdom Come rather than to Kingdom Gone?"[4] All civilized minds must pray that the unthinkable horror will never become fact. If there is any sense in which God himself prays, he must surely pray with us about this. But there will never be a God's Kingdom Gone. His kingdom is bombproof. Those who sincerely pray "Thy kingdom come" trust that his kingdom is coming and will come despite all the powers of hell. There is no atom that Death's power can render void. While we have time, we must do all we can to preserve this good earth and all that lives in it as it comes from the Father's hands. I want to be the last person on earth to say or do anything that might encourage an indifferent and irresponsible attitude toward this most terrible menace of our years. Nevertheless, all who believe that God is true must stand with Martin Luther as he proclaims, in *Ein feste Burg,* that "His kingdom is forever."

In 1860 a French chemist named Marcellin Berthelot prophesied: "Within a hundred years of physical and chemical science man will know what the atom is. It is my belief that when science reaches this stage, God will come down to earth with his big ring of keys and will say to humanity, 'Gentlemen, it's closing time!' "[5] This image of God aptly suggests the truth that God is complete master of the scenes, *all* scenes and scenarios, on earth no less than in heaven.

The New Testament writers distinguish between life and death in spiritual terms, such as, for example, "He that loveth not his brother abideth in death."[6] "He that hath the Son hath life; and he that hath not the Son of God hath not life."[7] "To be carnally minded is death; but to be spiritually minded is life and peace."[8] These writers are speaking literally about life and death in these statements, and they expect us to understand them literally. They do not equate death with the death of the body nor life with the animation of the physical body, and neither should we.

We *exist* in God because God created us, and his creations, unlike our constructions, are all of them indestructible. We *live* when, already existing in God, we awaken to an awareness of who and what we are: God's children, called to be not only creatures but agents and servants of his love. To live is to participate in God's love for himself and for his whole creation, our own selves included. We cannot love God and love our neighbor without loving ourselves.

Every existence exists forever in God. Even the evil, the ugly, the false, the useless people and things? That question is in fact a statement, and once it is seen as a statement it raises a counterquestion: *Who says* that some person or thing is evil, ugly, false, or useless? Is anybody under God, and other than God, competent to judge? Of this, more later.

God's Holy Spirit, Brontë says, "animates eternal years" and "changes, sustains, dissolves, creates, and rears." We are to see all of the world in God as undergoing this constant change and development toward God's goal which he has in mind for each creature and for all creation together. There is change and there is sustaining, there is dissolution as there is creation, and through it all there is *rearing*. What a wonderful word in this context! Everybody, everything that exists in God is being reared. When William James turned seventy, somebody asked him if he believed in personal immortality. "Never strongly," he replied, "but more so as I grow older." "And why is that?" "Because I'm just getting fit to live."[9]

It was a pleasantry, yet seriously meant. James was testifying to a deep sense that over all his years he was being reared by Somebody for some purpose beyond his own ken. He knew himself well enough to realize that for all his maturity of mind and spirit he was in fact, at seventy, just getting fit to live. Anybody with a true self-awareness must share this feeling. Whether or not it is a valid pointer toward personal immortality is a proper matter for debate. I know that some wise people who share this feeling of being "reared" do not consider it an intimation of immortality. With my own trust in the validity of my passionate intuition I cannot imagine what could be said on the negative side that would make any sense to me, but of course that could be just my ignorance.

If all people, all creatures, all things eternally subsist in God, and if, as I fear we must acknowledge without argument, God's human creatures can defy God's will for them and refuse to be servant-children of his love, how then are we to distinguish in our thinking between those sheep and those goats in God? For years I have been groping around for some simple formulation of this distinction. At last I came upon the exactly right one, not surprisingly in the writings of C. S. Lewis. In his *Preface to Paradise Lost* he writes: "Those who will not be God's sons become his tools."[10] Some twenty-six centuries ago God spoke that truth to us the through a Hebrew prophet whose countrymen, God's chosen but disobedient people, were being terribly ravaged by the Assyrians, a people savage, cruel, and ungodly. God cried, through the lips of Isaiah: "O Assyrian, the rod of mine anger, and the staff in their hand is mine indignation!"[11] The Assyrian was not a son of God. He was a tool of God, a whip in God's hand for the chastisement of God's faithless and rebellious people.

The Hebrew was a son of God in a sense that the Assyrian was not—*at least not yet.* Of that, more later. Was the Black Plague a tool of God? Adolf Hitler? Josef Stalin? Is cancer? Any kind of pat answer to this dreadful question must seem either blasphemous or insane. I will try not to make it pat when we come to it; but I do believe that, granted our premise, it is *simple,* and there is a world of difference between what is pat and what is simple.

NOTES

1. St. Augustine, *The City of God,* XIV, 28.
2. Ephesians 2:12.
3. Luke 20:38.
4. *The Asheville Citizen,* 29 June 1983.
5. Quoted in *The New York Times,* 2 October 1970.

6. 1 John 3:14b.
7. 1 John 5:12.
8. Romans 8:2.
9. Henry James, *The Letters of Henry James,* ed. Henry James, Jr. (New York: Atlantic Monthly Press, 1920).
10. C. S. Lewis, *A Preface to Paradise Lost* (London: Oxford University Press, 1942), p. 68.
11. Isaiah 10:5.

FIVE

"BRIGHT SHOOTS OF EVERLASTINGNESS"

Fool! All that is, at all,
Lasts ever, past recall;
Earth changes, but thy soul and God stand sure:
What entered into thee,
That was, is, and shall be:
Time's wheel runs back or stops; Potter and clay endure.
                Robert Browning, *Rabbi Ben Ezra.*

The following are ponderabilia from several sources widely differing in time, place, belief, and spirituality. I suggest that we try to listen to them in a receptive rather than an argumentative mood.

(1) From Henry Vaughan (1622–1695), "The Retreat":

Happy those early days, when I
Shined in my angel-infancy!
Before I understood this place
Appointed for my second race,
Or taught my soul to fancy aught
But a white celestial thought;
When yet I had not walked above
A mile or two from my first love,
And looking back, at that short space,

> *Could see a glimpse of his bright face;*
> *When on some gilded cloud, or flower*
> *My gazing soul would dwell an hour,*
> *And in those weaker glories spy*
> *Some shadow of eternity;*
> *Before I taught my tongue to wound*
> *My conscience with a sinful sound,*
> *Or had the black heart to dispense*
> *A several sin to every sense,*
> *But felt through all this fleshly dress*
> *Bright shoots of everlastingness.*

(2) From William Wordsworth (1770–1850), "Intimations of Immortality from Recollections of Early Childhood":

> *The Soul that rises with us, our life's Star,*
> *Hath had elsewhere its setting,*
> *And cometh from afar:*
> *Not in entire forgetfulness,*
> *And not in utter nakedness,*
> *But trailing clouds of glory do we come*
> *From God, who is our home:*
> *Heaven lies about us in our infancy!*
> *Shades of the prison-house begin to close*
> *Upon the growing Boy,*
> *But he beholds the light, and whence it flows,*
> *He sees it in his joy;*
> *The Youth, who daily farther from the east*
> *Must travel, still is Nature's Priest,*
> *And by the vision splendid*
> *Is on his way attended;*
> *At length the Man perceives it die away,*
> *And fade into the light of common day.*

(3) From Ralph Waldo Emerson (1803–1882), *Journals:*

A sleeping child gives me the impression of a traveler from a far country.

(4) From Arthur Schopenhauer (1788–1860), *The World as Will and Idea:*

> Every new-born being indeed comes fresh and blithe into the new existence, and enjoys it as a free gift: but its fresh existence is paid for by a worn-out existence which had perished, but which contained the indestructible seed out of which this new existence has arisen: they are one being. To show the bridge between the two would certainly be the solution of a great riddle.

Vaughan and Wordsworth consider the human infant a visitor from eternity who is still happily aware of his first home and his first love, before there sets in that education in corruption that we call growing up and is in truth growing away. When the infant gazes upon a bright cloud or flower it is as if its beauty has always hitherto been his environment. His coo of delight is the coo of recognition. He is not entirely forgetful of God his Home, whence he has come into this strange new place.

Most of us, watching a sleeping baby, must have had the feeling expressed by Emerson.

Schopenhauer, famed for his pessimism, rightly observes that every fresh existence comes by the self-sacrifice and death of its progenitors. That is the plain material fact of the matter. But when he says that the dead progenitor and the living offspring are "one being" he declares, whether intentionally or not, that the "dead" not only live in the living but that they are in truth one being. He thinks that if he could find the bridge between the two it would solve a great riddle. If my conviction is right, that all existence consists of being in God, there is no riddle.

Vaughan's word "shoot" in "bright shoots of everlastingness" has a splendid ambiguity, with two clear meanings combined. A shoot is a branch or twig from a living parent trunk, an offshoot. Or it is a flash or a twinge, like a twinge of pain or a flash of brightness. In Vaughan's phrase both meanings are present. As an infant he knew himself to be shot through with the brightness of the Home from whom he had come. Reflecting upon it in later years he came to see himself as a ray, a beam, of an eternal life in God.

We *have,* and we *are,* bright shoots of everlastingness. We must not overload the word "bright" in applying it to ourselves. Most of us most of the time do not see ourselves as radiantly bright, mentally, spiritually, or morally, any more than we are handsome if male or beautiful if female. The brightness of our being is to be seen more in our potentialities than in our actualities. You have some unusually high moment now and then, when your thinking or your doing rises high above your ordinary level, and you may exclaim delightedly, "I didn't know I had it in me!" It was the telltale brightness of what is both your primal and your ultimate being, your alpha and your omega. Its origin is in your prenatal past: "Trailing clouds of glory do we come/From God, who is our home!" Its end will be your completion, when God has finished his work of grace with you that we call growth. It may be that in eternity there will be no terminal end to your completion, that you will continue to rise from strength to strength and from glory to glory forever; but bear in mind that the word "end" means "purpose" as well as "stopping point."

It is a sad truth which Wordsworth observes, that the trails of glory disappear from our wake as we "grow up" in the miseducation this world provides for us. If this is the inescapable fate into which we are born, why does God put us through it? Heaven is our eternal home, heaven is our destination; we lost what we had when we entered this mortal life, we must regain what we have lost before we can reenter our immortal life. Has God sent us into this world on some pathetic errand like the Children's Crusade? I am sure not, because I trust my passionate intuition. It teaches me that we are incarnations of our eternal selves who exist in God, and that in our incarnations each one of us acquires a full personal identity. Before the worlds began I existed in the mind of God, and that means simply in God. On 14 April 1912 I became Carroll Eugene Simcox, who I shall be thenceforth and forever—for better or for worse. For better, I hope; that I wouldn't have missed it for anything, I know.

"And God breathed into his nostrils the breath of life, and man became a living soul."[1] When God breathes human life into us he incarnates us, makes us selves; individual selves, each with his own unique identity. There is only one you, and you are an eternal you; but until you were born you had not yet begun your active career as a self. What you get for all your pains in this "vale of misery" is your selfhood. John Keats called it "the vale of soul-making"[2] and that is exactly what it is. Soul-making means self-completion.

I don't care much for the word "soul." To most minds it suggests an entity apart from the body, an ethereal something that can cheerfully leave its body and live happily forever after without it. This is good Greek thinking; it is not good Christian thinking.

Nor do I care for the word "person," though I realize that we are permanently stuck with it. It doesn't really belong in our language except as a theological term to identify the Persons of the Holy Trinity. That is how it got into our Western languages, from the Latin *persona* meaning the mask the actor wore in ancient drama. It has a prissy, artificial sound even after all these years of vernacular use. Somebody says, "Who is this *person* who presumes to bore me by interrupting my session of sweet silent thought?" "Oh, *that* person!" To the fastidiously snooty, all the rest of us are not people but persons.

The good straightforward Anglo-Saxon word we want is *self.* My self is the whole I. It uses my body, mind, and spirit as the sacramental signs of my identity.

"We are not alone," wrote Paul Claudel. "To be born is for each man a getting to know. Every birth is a getting to know."[3] Getting to know isn't simply a matter of acquiring information about this and that; it is the primal birth to consciousness which is self-awareness, other-awareness, and God-awareness. To *know* is to feel as well as to reason, to experience the emotions and sensations as well as the intellect. God incarnates us so that we shall experience all this. Until we do, we cannot become his children of the kind he wants, and if you want to know why we can't you will have to ask him. We must become apelike before we can become God-like. No doubt it is as simple as that, to God; it doesn't seem so simple to many of us. It would be so if we were not so stuffy and conceited about our human dignity among the animals. In the minds of many (and let each examine his own) there is some resentment that God has not made us more like the angels and less like the animals. I addressed a letter to Charles Darwin on this subject in a little book titled *Notes to the Overworld,* [4] and I cannot make my present point better than by quoting what I wrote to him:

> You had to endure in your lifetime, and since, an unconscionable amount of senseless ridicule from Christian people who failed to understand your ideas, and failed also to appreciate your spirit of humble and courageous truthfulness. In your *Descent of Man* (why didn't you call it *Ascent of Man?*) you said: "We must acknowledge, it seems to me, that man with all his noble qualities still bears in his bodily frame the indelible stamp of his lowly origin." There seems to me nothing shameful in coming from a lowly origin, and I am astounded by the snappishness of Christians—of all people—who detest the thought of it. One would think it all the better cause to glorify the God who "raiseth up the poor out of the dust, and lifteth the needy out of the dung hill" (Psalm 113:7). The things we have to be ashamed of do not pertain to our "bodily frame" at all. As physical creatures of God we emerged from the primordial slime because he raised us from it. We have created a spiritual slime of our own in which to wallow. *This* is the infamy.

Benjamin Disraeli spoke foolishness at least once in his life. In an address to a diocesan conference of the Church of England he turned to the bishop who was presiding and said: "Is man an ape or an angel? I, my lord, am on the side of the angels. I repudiate with indignation and abhorrence these newfangled theories.''[5] The remark was stupid, for no reputable scientist ever said that man is an ape and no reputable theologian ever said that man is an angel. Disraeli was simply reacting, as does unregenerate humanity as a whole, against recognizing what Darwin called man's lowly origin. God is of quite another mind, and we do well to accept his dispensation without cavil. He wants us to be his servant-children who emerged first from the slime and then from the jungle, and who in our ascent have never lost that down-to-earth common touch of our animal ancestors and our collateral cousins. Our poor relations they may be, but we might as well accept them because we must share a common inheritance through all eternity.

NOTES

1. Genesis 2:7.
2. Letter to George and Georgiana Keats, 21 April 1819.
3. Paul Claudel, *Traité de la connaisance du monde.*
4. Carroll E. Simcox, *Notes to the Overworld* (New York: Seabury Press, 1972), p. 33.
5. Speech at Oxford Diocesan Conference, 25 November 1864.

SOULS/SELVES

> The soul is not where it lives but where it
> loves.
>
> Thomas Fuller, *Gnomologia*

Somebody who read the first draft of this book remarked, after reading the preceding chapter: "Maybe you'd better explain at more length why you want to replace the word *soul* with *self*. A lot of people have got used to *soul* and to them it is a beautiful word even though they can't tell you precisely what it means. And *self* has got itself associated in everybody's mind with egotism and selfishness."

Maybe I better had.

William James, around the turn of the century, said that souls have outlived their usefulness. He was speaking as a philosopher and psychologist, and he had in mind the idea of soul as a metaphysical entity, as distinct from body as a physical entity. "John Brown's body lies a-mold'ring in the grave, but his soul goes marching on." What does that say to you? It may say that the noble cause, the ideal of freedom for all men that Brown lived and died for, did not die with him but goes marching on in the world. Or it may say that although the ex-body, now the corpse, of Brown is rotting in the grave, the real, quintessential Brown survives because, being immortal in its essence, it couldn't die even if it tried. It was this latter idea of soul that James had in mind when he said that it had outlived its usefulness.

Many, probably most of us grew up with the idea that a human being is a mortal body with an immortal soul or, as a variant form of the same idea, that a person is an immortal soul inhabiting and expressing itself through a mortal body. In this concept body and soul are temporary partners, fellow travelers in a most literal and intimate sense of the phrase. At the end of your mortal career, body and soul separate. Your body goes down to the unending banquet of worms, not as a guest of honor but as *pièce de résistance,* while your soul (we hope) soars off to a somewhat Christianized version of Homer's Olympus where the blessed gods are happy all their days.

Ages ago, somebody wrote a doggerel Latin verse *(Animula vagula blandula)* and attributed it to poor Emperor Hadrian, who being dead was powerless to prevent the attribution. As Latin poetry it is wretched, but years ago I came upon a translation of it by an Englishman named Geoffrey Household. It charmed me so much that I memorized it, but neglected to memorize the actual source, i.e., the book in which it appeared. I apologize, Mr. Household, but I know it was yours, and it is beautiful, and I must now share it with my readers because it's too lovely to keep. The poet is contemplating the eventual parting of the ways of his soul and body, and he speaks to his soul thus:

> Odd little comrade, comfortable guest,
> Capricious, elfin puff of air,
> You're off! But where?
> And when you've left this breast,
> Tense little traveler, pale and bare,
> Will you find anything to laugh at there?

To my knowledge there never was a more exquisite expression than that of the old and almost universal concept of the body-soul partnership. But it has outlived its usefulness, if indeed it ever had any, largely by outliving its credibility.

As a Christian I am not supposed to agree with much that Bertrand Russell wrote in *Why I Am Not a Christian,* and in fact I don't, but on this point I think he is right as a ribstone pippin. He wrote:

> Believers in immortality will object to physiological arguments, such as I have been using, on the ground that soul and body are totally disparate, and that the soul is quite other than its empirical manifestations through our bodily organs. I believe this to be a metaphysical superstition. Mind and matter alike are for certain purposes convenient terms but are not ultimate realities. Electrons and protons, like the soul, are logical fictions; each is really a history, a series of events, not a single persistent entity. In the case of the soul, this is obvious from the facts of growth. Whoever considers conception, gestation, and infancy cannot seriously believe that the soul is an indivisible something, perfect and complete throughout this process. It is evident that it grows like the body, and that it derives both from the spermatozoon and from the ovum, so that it cannot be indivisible. This is not materialism: it is merely the recognition that everything interesting is a matter of organization, not of primal substance.[1]

I would like to ask Lord Russell what the spermatozoon and the ovum derive from, ultimately, but because he was a consistent and thoroughgoing atheist I'm sure that his answer would not be the Christian one. He was (I think) wrong about God but right about souls. If we think about souls, not as indivisible primal substance, which by its very nature has existed and will exist forever, but as *personal becomings,* we shall be able to go on using the word as a synonym for *selves.* Our selves/souls are *we in the making.* We are not human beings but human becomings. It is as one of our poets has said: "Man partly is, and wholly hopes to be." We are, if you like (or even if you don't), *events,* happenings; except that we don't "just happen" but are happenings in God. When Keats called this "just happen" but are happenings in God. When Keats called this world the vale of soul-making he clearly meant the vale of self-making, but because he was a poet and also a child of his age the word that came to his mind was soul, and I admit that his phrase sounds prettier.

We need to give some consideration to biblical teaching on this subject. Miller Burrows, a modern authority on biblical theology, observes: "Traditional Christianity has always been concerned with the salvation of the soul, but in the Bible the words translated 'soul' have by no means the same associations and implications as the English word."[2] The Hebrew word is *nephesh* and the Greek word is *psyche*.

The primary meaning of *nephesh* is "breath." It is because man has *nephesh* in him that he is a "living soul," according to Genesis 2:7 in the King James Version. But in Job 41:21 we read about the *nephesh* of the crocodile. Man and crocodile both have the same thing—*nephesh;* therefore both live. No doubt, man has something that makes him superior in God's order to the crocodile, but whatever that thing is it cannot be *nephesh*. In our traditional thought and speech man "has a soul" and the crocodile has not. But the Bible itself does not bear this out. Man's superiority lies in his having the image and likeness of God, not in having *nephesh*.

Burrows points out that "both *nephesh* and *psyche* frequently mean simply 'life' and are so translated."[3] And sometimes these words are best translated as "person." "Closely related to the meanings 'life' and 'person' is the meaning of 'self.' Thus 'my soul' means I, me, myself, etc."[4] In sum: in biblical language "soul" and "self" are synonymous, and the categorical distinction between them that we conventionally make is, to say the least, without any warrant of Holy Writ.

So let's agree, then, that throughout the rest of this exploration we will use the words "soul" and "self" interchangeably, as meaning exactly the same thing. Because I prefer "self" I will introduce our next reflection by saying that I am concerned about what happens to my self both now and when I die. Here is a statement by Teilhard de Chardin with which I must take some issue:

In itself, to be frank, the problem of personal survival does not worry me greatly. Once the fruit of my life has been gathered up into an immortality, a self-centered consciousness of that fact or enjoyment of it matters little to me. I can say in all sincerity that my personal happiness means nothing to me. It is enough for me in that respect that what is best in me should pass, there to remain forever, into one who is greater and finer than I.[5]

That sentiment is nobly unselfish. I have no doubt of Father Teilhard's total veracity when he says that his personal happiness means nothing to him, but I would raise with him the question, purely *en passant,* as to whether such a thing as our capacity for personal happiness, a gift of God, is something that we should value so lightly. Like him, I do not worry greatly, or even at all, about "the problem of personal survival." For me there is no problem, in the sense of a difficulty. Rather, I am concerned about the character and quality of my life now and at the moment when God will require it of me at my death.

When Father Teilhard speaks of how the best in himself may pass into one who is greater and finer than he I am reminded of the great philosophers of "process" in our age, notably Whitehead and Hartshorne. They see God himself as growing and evolving with his creation. I cannot accept their ultimate premise about God's relationship to his creation, but I gratefully acknowledge that through my study of their writings God is enlarging and clarifying my concept of how he makes eternal use of the best things we do in this present life for the continuing creation of his eternal world. Therefore I agree with Teilhard, and most happily, that what is best in me passes into God, "there to remain forever."

But he doesn't care very much whether *he himself,* Pierre Teilhard de Chardin, a man of flesh living in space-time when he wrote those words, passes into God along with the best in him when he dies. He died in 1955. I trust that among the first lessons he learned in God his eternal Home is that God cares, perhaps more than do we ourselves, about our "personal happiness," which is our personal fulfillment and completion, and for that reason will not allow us to be dropouts from existence.

I want myself, me, to follow both the best and the worst of me into God. This text comes to mind: "And I heard a voice from heaven saying unto me, write: Blessed are the dead who die in the Lord from henceforth: Yes, saith the Spirit, that they may rest from their labors; and their works do follow them."[6] According to this vision we do not follow our fruits and works into God; they follow us. This is how it should be and must be in the wise providence of God.

The works, the fruits, of your life while you are in the flesh are actually you yourself: you in action, you being and doing. You and what you do are one entity, not two. Shakespeare's sonnets are Shakespeare. Bach's music is Bach. The self and its fruits, be what they may, are as organically one as the tomato plant and the tomatoes it bears. At any rate, so it is in this world as we know it. What real reason have we to suppose that God will separate them at our death? And since he is not only our Creator but our Father, can it be that he wants our "fruits" to love and cherish forever but not us ourselves?

If God loves us as our Father, he wants our selves to be his forever. And our selves cannot be selves unless they are conscious: God-conscious, other-conscious, self-conscious. Father Teilhard, and the "process" theologians generally, seem to expect an extinction of personal consciousness at death. I expect an inconceivable heightening and enhancement of it. Because God is our Father he wills to use us as his servant-children in his working toward the completion of his creation, even as he does with us while we are here. This is the glory we share with him now and shall share with him forever.

"The soul is but a hollow which God fills," as Lewis says.[7] We grow in being as God feeds and fills us with the life eternal. He fills this "hollow" so that we can love him and join him in loving his world, as servants of that love in worlds we have not yet traversed and which may still be waiting to be born.

NOTES

1. Bertrand Russell, *Why I Am Not a Christian* (London: George Allen & Unwin, Ltd., 1957), p. 52.
2. Millar Burrows, *An Outline of Biblical Theology* (Philadelphia: The Westminster Press, 1946), p. 134.
3. Ibid., p. 135.
4. Ibid., p. 136.
5. Pierre Teilhard de Chardin, *Christianity and Evolution* (London: William Collins Sons & Company, Ltd., 1969), p. 115.
6. Revelation 14:13.
7. C. S. Lewis, *The Problem of Pain* (New York: The Macmillan Company, 1962), p. 151.

SEVEN

THE STAR AND
THE DANDELION

A handful of sand is an anthology of the universe.
David McCord

G. K. Chesterton as a young journalist once got himself into trouble with his editor. A man named Grant Allen had written a book on the subject of the evolution of the idea of God. Chesterton remarked that a book by God on the evolution of the idea of Grant Allen would be much more interesting. The editor thought the suggestion was blasphemous. Chesterton felt that the title of Allen's book was the real blasphemy, for it meant, when translated into English, "I will show you how this nonsensical idea that there is a God grew up among men."

You are an idea in the mind of God, and that is why you have existed from all eternity and will exist to all eternity. It's as simple as that. But the simplicity of God is far beyond our poor human complexity to imagine. I quote Chesterton again: "A lady I know picked up a book of selections from St. Thomas Aquinas, with a commentary; and began hopefully to read a section with the innocent heading, 'The Simplicity of God.' She then laid down the book with a sigh and said, 'Well, if that's His simplicity, I wonder what His complexity is like.' "[1]

As we get into this indispensable chapter we recall Emerson's dictum that we are symbols and we inhabit symbols. Everything in us, everything in this world, is a temporal, spatial, finite symbol of something eternal in God. The immensity of the universe symbolizes God's immensity, his infinite capacity that contains all of creation. He contains everything, he is contained by nothing. The splendor of a golden sunset symbolizes the Divine Beauty. Our mind is at once a symbol and an instrument of God's mind. But the best of symbols never conveys more than a part of the truth it symbolizes. Our mind as a symbol of God's mind is only a pointer to what it symbolizes, in the way that the reflection of the sun that you see in a glittering dewdrop points you to the sun.

Our mind infinitely lacks the fullness and perfection of God's mind. An idea in your mind may give you an inkling of an idea in God's mind, but it is a very dim inkling at best. None of the problems that a good idea has to cope with in your mind can trouble an idea in God's mind. Suppose that you were a good idea in your mind and that you could think and speak independently. You would have constant occasion to complain thus: "Here I am, a first-rate idea as to what this self whose mind I inhabit ought to do. Unhappily I doubt that I shall ever be acted upon, or that I shall ever lead this self to exactly what I want to be my consequence. If only I could, I would gladly be to this self as is Jeeves to Bertie Wooster in Wodehouse's novels. But this self is either too lazy or too stupid to understand what I'm trying to tell him (or her) to do. I can only wait and see what becomes of me, but knowing as I do this Count (or Countess) of No Account, I fear the worst."

If you can't imagine an idea in your mind having such cause for complaint, imagine it to be in my mind, where its frustrations would be most grievous and beyond number.

An idea in our mind is the seed of a possibility, no more. In God's mind there is no interval whatever, and no difference or discontinuity, between the seed and the flower, the possibility and the actuality. "He spake, and it was done" says the Psalmist.[2] God says "Let there be"[3]—and it is so. An idea in a human mind must be acted upon or carried out by another part of the human self. In God there are no "body, parts, or passions."[4] The mind of God *is* God. Whatever exists in that mind exists eternally as an idea in a human mind exists temporally, but with this world of difference: The whole world is within the mind of God and is entirely subject to it; therefore, there can be no separation or interval or even distinction between an idea of God and its fulfillment. There is no point, then, in saying that you are a fulfillment of an idea of God: You are that idea itself; the idea is you, because idea and fulfillment are one and the same. You are one of those existences of which Brontë speaks: Though earth and man were gone, and suns and universes ceased to be, and God were left alone, every existence would exist in him. Even you. Even I.

When God looks into his own mind, as he must constantly do, he sees everything that ever has existed or ever will exist. He sees each one separately and all of them together. He cherishes each thing with an everlasting love. He sees each and all in what we call their past, present, and future, but he sees them in their *totum simul,* the Eternal Now, their all-together-at-once-ness. Among all that he sees, loves, and rejoices in are you: as you have been, as you are, as you will be in that End to which there is no end.

What is true of human beings is no less true of angels and other rational creatures living in parts of God's creation of which we know nothing. Moreover, it is true not only of the more exalted creatures (as we measure worth and dignity) but of what we call the lower, baser, even "evil" creatures. I put "evil" in quotes to suggest that it is at least problematical whether a creature is evil simply because *we* think it is. God is the only judge of good and evil. If the mind of God is the mind of Christ, we may note that Jesus is not on record as having called anything evil, with two noteworthy exceptions: *devils* and *people like us.* To the latter he said: "If you, being evil, know how to give good gifts to your children, how much more shall your heavenly Father . . . ?"[5] If ever it is granted us to know as we are now known, we may well see that many things, possibly all things, that we now call evil were not evil at all; that they were perhaps inconvenient or troubling to us at a time when we were incapable of seeing the creation in its wholeness.

Having noted in the last paragraph that Jesus called devils and people like us evil, we need to give a thought to this. If devils and human beings are all creatures of God, how can they be evil? When we take into account all of the recorded words and deeds of Jesus I think we find clearly implicit in them all the answer that he would give us, namely, that every creature born of God's love that has rebelled against and rejected that love is now in a state of dis-grace, an evil condition. It is no longer its true self. It must arise and return to its Father. If and when it does, it will shed its garment of dis-grace, its evil, and become once again what it was from its beginning.

The world as a whole, with every creature in it, has a single and common destiny. Each creature, from the highest archangel down to the lowliest pebble, has its particular individual destiny that, like the universal one, is eternal because it is fulfilled in God.

The term "destiny" has always seemed to me an essentially pagan word rather than Christian, like "fate" and "luck." But it is clear from the range of its use that most people have some sense of what they call destiny, and I do not doubt that what they sense is somehow real. Voltaire expressed a thought about this that I find fascinating, and it would be frightening if it did not contain a palpable flaw in its premise. He wrote: "If you could disturb the destiny of a fly, there would be nothing to stop you from controlling the destiny of all other flies, of all other animals, of all men, of all nature. You would find yourself in the end more powerful than God."[6] My fright vanishes upon reflection that if the fly's destiny is really its destiny there is no way that any presumptuous mortal could ever disturb it: For what can be disturbed by any creature is not destiny. (In justice to Voltaire, he was speaking hypothetically and began his statement with "If.")

There is a Christian concept of destiny and it is this: Destiny is whatever is willed by God. God's will is the creation's destiny, and the creature's.

There's a divinity that shapes our ends,
Rough-hew them how we will.[7]

But isn't that downright predestination? You may well ask, and I'm not sure I can as well answer. I am reluctant to own to being a predestinarian because in historic theology that term normally means that your every thought, word, or deed, be it good or bad, is not really your own at all because God has forced it on you. When this traditional concept of predestination is pushed to its logical conclusion it declares that you are a helpless puppet dancing on strings manipulated by that divinity that shapes our ends. If the divinity wants you to act either the hero or the villain in his cosmic Punch-and-Judy show, that is what you will be. On that principle, Judas was not accountable for what he did: God forced him to do it. Because I find this idea both unconvincing and abhorrent I eschew the label normally attached to it.

The destiny of the fly, the destiny of Judas, the destiny of you or me, is already known to God, and it is willed by God, and it is now in process of being worked out. It does not work itself out as an ineluctable impersonal force; God and we work it out together. "We know that in everything God works for good with those who love him, who are called according to his purpose."[8] When we love God and serve him as his children and agents of his love, we are given assurance as we go that we are fulfilling our eternal destiny; we are actually living it out. But we cannot see our destiny's final shape. We only know that its "glory shall be revealed in us."[9]

Voltaire was right in his intuition that all creatures, man and fly together, share a common destiny, so that to control the destiny of one would be to control the destiny of all. Thank God, man cannot control the destiny of the fly and thus bring the whole universe to smash. Man can swat and kill the fly but he cannot revise its destiny.

The truth Voltaire had in mind is better expressed in these lines of Francis Thompson:

> *All things by immortal power*
> *Near or far,*
> *Hiddenly*
> *To each other linkèd are,*
> *That thou canst not stir a flower*
> *Without troubling of a star.*[10]

Earlier, in chapter two, reference was made to a star known to astronomers as Ross 248. After Pioneer 10 travels some 32,000 years it will come within 3.3 light years of that star. It all seems a rather far piece down the heavenly way. But go out into your yard and pluck one dandelion and you "trouble" Ross 248. That is the poet's way of saying that the dandelion and the star have a common destiny in which they are members one of another, and that this destiny is *now* because it is *eternal*. Far apart though they are both spatially and topically, in the mind of God, i.e., in God, in reality, they are closer to each other than breathing, nearer than hands and feet. Because they exist in God it is the destiny of all created things to share such closeness and unity from everlasting to everlasting.

To make my point I chose a dandelion rather than a rose, for a reason. Everybody loves a rose, nobody loves a dandelion—except God. And we shall not be ready for our full fruition and maturity as children of God, we shall not be completely "saved," until we love dandelions, and all other creatures we find hard to love, as God loves them.[11] Somebody who worked for the U.S. Department of Agriculture some years ago gave some advice that was good not only horticulturally but theologically. He was responding to a letter that ran something like this: "I have tried everything I have heard about, including advice in your bulletins, on how to get rid of dandelions, and I still have them. What is left for me?" Came this inspired reply: "If you have tried everything to get rid of dandelions and you still have them, only one course is left to you: learn to love them."

The implications of that counsel run far beyond lawns and gardens. We must learn to love everybody and everything with whom and which we share life in God—our eternal Home and theirs.

NOTES

1. G. K. Chesterton, *Saint Thomas Aquinas* (New York: Sheed and Ward, 1933), p. xi.
2. Psalm 33:9.
3. Genesis 1:3, *et passim.*
4. Articles of Religion, i, Book of Common Prayer.
5. Matthew 7:11.
6. Voltaire, *Philosophical Dictionary,* "Destiny."
7. Shakespeare, *Hamlet,* I, ii, 10.
8. Romans 8:28, Revised Standard Version. This is a correct translation. The Authorized Version's reading, "all things work together for good to them that love God," is incorrect and badly misleading. "Things" do not work; they have to be worked.
9. Romans 8:18.
10. Francis Thompson, "The Mistress of Vision."
11. This is a personal note to Billie, who most graciously and helpfully read this book in manuscript. You ask: "How do you know? How about snakes which I loathe and which epitomize evil to me?" I answer: I know by the intuition of faith that God, the infinitely good, creates all things, therefore every creature is originally and intrinsically good and *cannot* be evil. And yes, you must get over your loathing of snakes, as I must get over mine, and start loving them, so you might as well go to work on it now, because the sooner you get it done the better it will be for both you and the snakes. "The leopard shall lie down with the kid" (Isaiah 11:6), and you will revel in the beauty of the water snakes—as did Coleridge's ancient mariner after he had "blessed them unaware."

EIGHT

SALVATION FROM BOORISHNESS

It is a strange thing to come home.
While yet on the journey, you cannot at all
realize how strange it will be.
Selma Lagerlöf, *The Miracles of Antichrist*

From our conception onward, our life is a homeward journey full of things wonderful and fearful. Before we were born we were not only at home in God but at home *with* God in a kind of fetal comfort. But that was easy: We were not yet conscious, or at most only rudimentarily so. Birth is awakening to consciousness, and once born we are conscious forever. Being conscious, we find our home-going strange and we may find Home even stranger when we arrive. That will depend, no doubt, upon how much of our sense of strangeness we overcome, by God's grace, while on our journey. There is paradox here, and the supreme poet of paradox celebrates it in these lines:

> *This world is wild as an old wives' tale,*
> *And strange the plain things are.*
> *The earth is enough and the air is enough*
> *For our wonder and our war;*

But our rest is as far as the fire-drake swings
And our peace is put in impossible things
Where clashed and thundered unthinkable wings
Round an incredible star.[1]

If our eternal home in God is so strange to us, how can we consider it home at all? Is not home a place where you put your feet up on the table when you feel like it, and order your wife (or husband) around, and your children (or parents),[2] and curse the boss whom you dare not curse at the office? In short, can't we be *comfortable* at home, just as we are, doing what comes naturally?

We can find no warrant in the Gospel for a comfortable reply to that question. Our eternal Home will not be altered to match our present life-style. All the alterations must be made in ourselves. This is what the Way called Christianity is all about: making the alterations that will fit us for life at Home.

No finer word about home was ever spoken than this by Emerson: "Let a man behave in his own house as a guest."[3] Here and now we are guests in the Father's house of the many mansions[4] and our Father wants us to be joyful in it, but he does not want us to behave as boors. The strangeness of our homeward journey and of our Home Himself is solely the result of our present boorishness. "We find ourselves out of sympathy with God from the start,"[5] as one theologian puts it. We are out of sympathy with him in much the same way that a musical boor is out of sympathy with Beethoven.

There are far worse things than boorishness, and we are all guilty of at least some of them. A boor may be a diamond in the rough; indeed, to God he undoubtedly is. But he is one who, as of now, is not ready for the higher and finer life for which he is created.

Twenty-five centuries ago Sappho of Lesbos wrote a tender little ode to Hesperus, the evening star: "You bring home the creatures that bright Dawn scattered—the sheep, the goat, the child to its mother." To those creatures, the child included, home is not at all strange. But to "mature" human beings, mature in what we call normal and natural life, God is strange and the road to him strange.

How strange, and in what ways strange, can readily be seen by reviewing the Sermon on the Mount in chapters five through seven of St. Matthew's Gospel. Where will you find stranger, less congenial doctrine than in those dominical words that we have not yet assimilated after all these centuries? "Blessed are the poor in spirit." "Blessed are the meek." "Blessed are the persecuted for righteousness' sake." "Whosoever shall say, Thou fool, shall be in danger of hell fire." "Whosoever shall smite thee on thy right cheek, turn to him the other also." "Love your enemies, bless them that curse you, do good to them that hate you, and pray for them that despitefully use you, and persecute you, *that ye may be the children of your Father in heaven. . . .*"

In those words I have italicized we see the reason for the strangeness of these counsels to us. This is not human goodness Jesus is talking about, but divine—and we are only human. God through Christ calls us to be not man-like but God-like. Only by striving to become so while we are here in the vale of soul-making can we become ready for life at Home as no longer boorish strangers but children of our Father "to the manner born."

"Goodness is not felicity but the road thither,"[6] said a Christian pilgrim of the seventeenth century. God prepares us for our homecoming by showing us in Jesus the pattern to which our lives must be increasingly conformed as we journey. About this, it may be well to reconsider one of everybody's favorite parables (Luke 15:11–36) to note something that it does *not* teach. Reading this story of a man with two sons, most of us easily identify with the younger one who squandered his inheritance foolishly, then came to himself, then went home to cast himself upon his father's mercy. It is, as we read it, a happy ending, at least for the boy. What happened after father and son and the whole household enjoyed the glorious homecoming party we are not told, for that is not at all what the story is about. But we need to see it not as a happy ending but as a happy beginning, a happy new beginning, a happy renewal of shared life with God that had been broken off. "This, thy brother, was dead, and is alive *again*," says the father. Forgiveness restores what was dead.

The forgiven one is alive again, and resurrection in the present makes possible life in the future.

When our Father receives and welcomes us as we turn to him, it is to make something of us as his sons and daughters: specifically, to make us junior partners in his continuing creation of his world. We live in an incomplete world and we are very incomplete ourselves, but God has high plans for us. "Do ye not know that the saints shall judge the world?" asks St. Paul.[7] He goes on to say that the saints, meaning all who are being fitted to live at Home, are to judge even the angels. We may be called to even more exalted tasks than judging men and angels. Whatever it is, it is no work for boors. If we are to be of any use to God, here or hereafter, we must be reared to it by that saving strangeness which is the theme of the Sermon on the Mount.

As we strive to live by the pattern shown to us by Jesus we find that, however hard it continues to be, it does make more and more sense as we go on. That is because, while we try to live up to our high and strange calling, the Lord who calls us gives us increasingly his own vision of things.

Our learning *to see as God sees* is the beginning of the end of our boorishness. As I ponder this, one of my favorite poems of Kipling— except for one word—comes to mind. The troubling word is in the last line.

When Earth's last picture is painted, and the tubes are twisted and dried,
When the oldest colors have faded, and the youngest critic has died,
We shall rest, and, faith, we shall need it—lie down for an aeon or two,
Till the Master of all good workmen shall put us to work anew.

And those that are good shall be happy: they shall sit in a golden chair;
They shall splash at a ten-league canvas with brushes of comets' hair.
They shall find real saints to draw from—Magdalene, Peter, and Paul;
They shall work for an age at a sitting and never be tired at all!

And only the Master shall praise us, and only the Master shall blame;

And no one shall work for money, and no one shall work for fame,
But each for the joy of the working, and each, in his separate star,
Shall draw the Thing as he sees It for the God of Things as They are![8]

Who am I to criticize this celebrated poet? Yet I am constrained to say it: "Shall draw the Thing as he sees It" would better read "Shall draw the Thing as God sees It." Until the artist sees the Thing as God sees It he is not yet a completed artist, he is not yet able to see the "things as they are."

"Blessed are the pure in heart, for they shall see God."[9] Purity of heart is that singleness in love that excludes all rivals. It is pure disinterestedness in loving God. When such is our love, we begin to see God as he is. Something humanly analogous would be in somebody's saying, "I could never see the glory of Homer until I learned enough Greek to be able to read him in the only language in which he can be read." It is what we mean when we say "Try it and see for yourself." The vision of God is given increasingly to those who, following Jesus as their only Master, begin to emerge from all the selfish, greedy, cramping qualities that characterize boorishness. Humility, meekness, compassion, hunger and thirst for a higher goodness, love for friend and foe alike—these qualities lose their strangeness as we grow into them. In fact, they lose their strangeness before they lose their hardness. They become fulfilling and satisfying. This means that Christ is getting on with his present task: to prepare us for Home, where we shall join those who "rest not day or night, saying, Holy, holy, holy, Lord God Almighty, which was, and is, and is to come,"[10] who "serve him day and night in his temple."[11]

That is the language of transcendental vision and we need not press it for a baldly literal meaning, but it clearly and rightly implies that they who are eternally at Home are no longer strangers to God, nor he to them. Their worship is their service, and it consists of being so conformed to God in character that they see what he sees and love what he loves.

"Beloved, now are we the sons of God, and it doth not yet appear what we shall be; but we know that, when he shall appear, we shall be like him, for we shall see him as he is."[12]

NOTES

1. G. K. Chesterton, from "The House of Christmas," in *The Collected Poems of Gilbert Keith Chesterton* (London: Burns, Oates & Washbourne, 1927), p. 123. By permission of Miss D. E. Collins.
2. "The thing that impresses me most about America is the way parents obey their children." Edward, Duke of Windsor, quoted in *Look,* 5 March 1957.
3. Emerson, *Journals.*
4. John 14:2. There is no reason why we must think of the Father's house and the many mansions as located in "the next world," as distinct from "this world." There is only one world, ultimately, and it is all the Father's house.
5. I have seen this statement attributed to E. J. Bicknell, an English theologian.
6. Sir Thomas Overbury, *News from Any Whence.*
7. 1 Corinthians 6:2.
8. Rudyard Kipling, "When Earth's Last Picture is Painted," from *Rudyard Kipling's Verse, Definitive Edition*, by Rudyard Kipling. Copyright 1892 to 1905 by Rudyard Kipling. Reprinted by permission of Doubleday and Company, Inc.
9. Matthew 5:8.
10. Revelation 4:8.
11. Revelation 7:15.
12. 1 John 3:2.

THE GLORY

The simplest peasant loving his cow is more
divine than the monarch whose monarchy is his glory.
George Macdonald, *Creation in Christ*

The learned and literary gentlemen who, by His Majesty's appoint-
ment, gave us what we know as the King James Version of the
Bible made remarkably few errors in translation, considering the
magnitude of their task and the corruptions in many parts of the
original text. They made one, however, which I tripped upon recently while looking for something else. This particular error is so
felicitous that I am bold to call it divinely inspired, and I know that
some would call my doing so not only bold but brazen. How dare
I suggest that God could inspire somebody to commit an error in
translating his sacred Word? I dare it only if I believe that in some
cases a mistranslation of a humanly written word may better convey
God's truth than a correct translation would, and in this case I so
believe.

The King James reading in question is Romans 8:18: "I reckon
that the sufferings of this present time are not worthy to be compared with the glory which shall be revealed in us." Those last two
words, "in us," are egregiously wrong as a translation of what Paul

59

wrote *(eis hēmas),* and eminently right as translation of what he would have written *(en hēmas)* if he had expressed himself more precisely. I say this because it is abundantly clear from such a passage as Galatians 1:16, where he speaks of how God had revealed his Son not *to* him but *in* him, that this was Paul's normal way of seeing and understanding divine revelation—as an inward vision rather than an outward one.

Why do you suppose the English translator, ca. 1610, "corrected" Paul? We can only guess, and in any case it is not at all germane to the point I wish to make about it. But I enjoy guessing and I have a fancy (a fantasy, if you insist) to share with you. The members of the royal commission of translators were God's Englishmen and scholars with a fine feel for language. One of them (this is my fancy) had been assigned Romans to put into English, and when he came to this spot in the text he mused: "Paul was an awfully decent sort of chap, you know, and bright too—for his time and place. But his Greek was barbarous. He'd never been to Oxford or Cambridge. After all, we can't all be British, now can we? So I'll give him a little help with this. I know what he *would* have said if he'd known his Greek as well as Sophocles did, or I do." So he kindly corrected Paul's "to us" to "in us." Presumptuous he may have been, but right. Perhaps God sometimes lets somebody be presumptuous and right, when truth is at stake, and appropriately punishes the presumption later on. "Shall not the Judge of all the earth do right?"[1]

You may wonder why I make such a fuss about a two-letter preposition. Then consider the difference between something that appears *to* you and something that appears *in* you. A falling star appears *to* you. If you were to say that it appears *in* you there would be some loving concern about your mental state. In the case now before us, that of the Glory yet to be revealed, the difference is infinite. If the Glory appears *to* us, we are only spectators of it. If it appears *in* us, we are a part of it and it is a part of us.

To be glorified is to be made glorious with the Glory itself, with what C. S. Lewis calls the "Glory Himself," meaning Christ.[2] To be glorified is to be Christified; to be Christified is to be drawn into the life of God while yet retaining our individual creaturely identities.

Our present sufferings are nothing compared to the Glory *we shall ourselves become.* A wonderful line of Shelley's after the death of Keats seems analogous: ''He is a portion of the loveliness/Which once he made more lovely.''[3] If the Glory is in us now, in any degree however slight, we shall become forever a portion of that Glory—again, however slight.

But what is this glory—*the* Glory? In trying to work out my own answer to this question I have recently reread C. S. Lewis's essay, originally delivered as a sermon, ''The Weight of Glory.'' It is very rich in precious insights, but it seems to me that it lacks a recognition of the stupendous paradox of the Glory—that its very essence is what the world considers disgraceful and contemptible. The Glory is the direct opposite of everything the wise world considers praiseworthy and desirable—in a word, glorious.

The writer of the First Epistle of Peter was trying to give encouragement to some of the first Christians, who were undergoing not only scorn and contumely but also cruel persecution by the world. Mark well how he expresses what I have called the stupendous paradox of the Glory: ''Beloved, think it not strange concerning the fiery trial which is to try you, as though some strange thing happened unto you: but rejoice, inasmuch as ye are partakers of Christ's sufferings; that, when his glory shall be revealed, ye may be glad with exceeding joy. If ye be reproached for the name of Christ, happy are ye; for *the spirit of glory and of God* resteth upon you. . . .''[4]

The spirit of glory and of God. Here this spirit of Christ the Suffering Servant of God and man, and of Christ's faithful followers in his Way of the Cross, is called the glory of God himself. That is the paradox—expressed in such phrases as the Crucified God.

George Macdonald tells us in the epigraph of this chapter that the simplest peasant loving his cow is more divine than the monarch whose monarchy is his glory. This peasant loving his cow is beginning to walk in the Glory—it is beginning to be revealed in him. Loving the cow is not at all simply his feeding her so that he can get her milk and eventually sell her to the butcher. It is, in a sense, playing God to her by caring for her. This loving peasant calls to mind the good shepherd of whom Jesus speaks as he explains his own relationship to the human race. The good shepherd is he who lays down his life for the sheep. Now, from a strictly economic point of view, such behavior is absurd, just as, from that point of view, it is absurd for a shepherd to leave ninety-nine of his sheep in the wilderness—an easy and helpless prey to predators—while he goes looking for the lost one. But of course what Jesus wants to impress upon us by such figures is that the Glory—"the spirit of glory *and of God*"—lies in this very absurdity. That is the spirit in which God creates and loves and rules—and dies, in the sense that all love is a dying to self. Somewhere in Blake's writings it is rightly observed that every little act of love is a death in the divine image. And that is the Glory.

"When we were yet without strength, in due time Christ died for the ungodly."[5] In a word, God in Christ loved us to his own death when we simply weren't worth a damn. That is the Glory as revealed by Christ in his sacrifice.

The Glory in any human life is love like that—the little death, the daily dying in the divine image. We must understand that God does not simply send his divine Son into our world to give us and to show us this Glory. God, as God, in his eternal and unutterable Glory, loves like that. God's own Cross is in every act of his creation.

In an unforgettable sermon on "The Riddle of Equality" Paul Tillich said this:

> It is the greatness and heart of the Christian message that God, as manifest in the Christ on the Cross, totally participates in the dying of a child, in the condemnation of the criminal, in the disintegration of a mind, in starvation and famine, and even in the human rejection of Himself. There is no human condition

into which the divine presence does not penetrate. That is what the Cross, the most extreme of all human conditions, tells us. The riddle of inequality cannot be solved on the level of our separation from each other. It is eternally solved through the divine participation in the life of all of us and every being. The certainty of divine participation gives us the courage to endure the riddle of inequality, although our finite minds cannot solve it.[6]

The Glory of God is seen in this present world in such manifestations as his dying on the Cross, his "participation" in the disintegration of a mind, and all such tragic events. It is not God who condemns the criminal or kills the child or inflicts starvation or plague upon a people. It is God who is condemned and suffers and dies with them and in them. Tillich does not define this divine participation in the woes of his world because it is beyond definition. It is the Glory, inscrutable and incomprehensible but the only ultimate reality of the world's existence. God's every creative act costs him his life, even though he never stays dead.

Our participation in the Glory is our voluntary reception and reflection of it in our own lives—our giving and self-dying love responding to his.

"We love, because he first loved us."[7] The King James reads "We love *him,* because he first loved us." But most of the best textual sources are against the "him" in the statement. We should understand it to say that if we receive and respond rightly to God's love for us and for every creature he has made we will love not only him but his whole creation, in each and in all its parts: love it as he loves it, *in the way, the spirit,* in which he loves it. When we do, truly "the spirit of Glory and of God resteth upon" us.

There is a section in Teilhard de Chardin's book *The Divine Milieu,* consisting of just three pages, to which I have been returning for meditation frequently over the past twenty years or so. It is labeled "The Meaning of the Cross" and it concludes with this challenging statement: "The Christian is not asked to swoon in the shadow, but to climb in the light, of the Cross."[8] According to Father Teilhard's reasoning, and mine, the Cross represents the conflict between the world God loves to his own death and God himself, with all those who share his Glory. Jesus was glorious and glorified in his dying because he was *able* to love to his death the world that crucified him. He was Christ the Victor on Calvary, and *not,* as in all too much traditional but thoroughly false atonement theology, Christ the Victim. By being lifted up on the Cross, rather than exercising his option of "playing it safe" by not loving the world as he did, he began to draw all men unto himself and hence into God, even as he predicted that he would.[9] God dying on the Cross is God creating. When we die to self that we may live to God we become, as St. Peter put it, partakers of Christ's sufferings, God's sufferings; and so doing we become participants in the Glory.

That Glory is now revealed whenever anybody loves and suffers that "little death in the divine image" which all loving is. But it has, as Paul said, yet to be revealed in us. It is most probable, practically certain, that what he had specifically in his mind and expectation when he wrote those words was an imminent divine and glorious catastrophe[10] in which the Glory would be fully manifested throughout all creation, in total triumph, so that no more crucifixions of God and his saints would be possible. We may or may not share that particular form of the expectation. But late or soon, in whatever form and shape God wills, that Glory is going to be fully and finally revealed *in* us, *through* us,—and, of course, *to* us.

The German poet Rainer Maria Rilke, in a letter to a young poet, made this arresting remark: "The future enters into us in order to transform itself in us, long before it happens."[11] I don't know quite what he meant about the future transforming itself in us, and in any case he was talking about the human and temporal future. We can borrow his metaphor and say that whenever we are enabled by God's grace to love in God's image, the Glory that is yet to be revealed enters into us to transform, not itself, but us. And we become proleptically citizens of eternity while yet pilgrims and strangers in this present world.

NOTES

1. Genesis 18:25.
2. C. S. Lewis, *The Weight of Glory* (New York: The Macmillan Company, 1949), p. 15.
3. Percy Bysshe Shelley, "Adonais: An Elegy on the Death of John Keats."
4. 1 Peter 4:12–14.
5. Romans 5:6.
6. Paul Tillich, *The Eternal Now* (New York: Charles Scribner's Sons, 1956), p. 46.
7. 1 John 4:19.
8. Pierre Teilhard de Chardin, *The Divine Milieu,* trans. Bernard Wall (New York: Harper & Row, Publishers, 1960), pp. 76–79.
9. John 12:32.
10. Bear in mind that a catastrophe may be either a glorious or a terrible event, depending upon whether you want it or you don't. It's just a total revolution.
11. Rainer Maria Rilke, *Letters to a Young Poet* (August 12, 1904), translated by M. D. Herter Norton (New York: Norton, 1963).

TEN

"A DARK, INSCRUTABLE WORKMANSHIP"

> Dust as we are, the immortal spirit grows
> Like harmony in music: there is a dark
> Inscrutable workmanship that reconciles
> Discordant elements, makes them cling together
> In one society. How strange, that all
> The terrors, pains, and early miseries,
> Regrets, vexations, lassitudes interfused
> Within my mind, should e'er have borne a part,
> And that a needful part, in making up
> The calm existence that is mine when I
> Am worthy of myself!
>   William Wordsworth, "The Prelude"

As long as we live we grow, though the self can grow downward as well as upward. People apparently grow regardless of whether or not they have any belief in divine grace. The unbeliever or the irreligious may say that we grow simply because that's life, and not because there is some "Power not ourselves"[1] that makes for growth. But anybody who believes in the God who creates will see healthy and beneficial growth as the work of God continuing his creation of a life. All good growth is God's work.

Wordsworth's lines I have quoted could be taken as an expression of a purely naturalistic idea of growth. In them God is not mentioned, nor are his workings noted or even implied except in the reference to "a dark inscrutable workmanship." Where there is workmanship there must perforce be a workman. Wordsworth was typically English in his reticence about God. A Frenchman[2] who spent some time in England earlier in this century wrote a book about the English, in the spirit of that admiration which is also wonderment. Among his observations was this: "The Englishman cultivates fog, and calls it reverence." So it seems to many non-English and to some English. It is how people like Wordsworth appear to others. He could speak copiously and reverently about Nature, and "Nature's holy plan,"[3] but he was exceedingly shy about God and God's holy plans. Perhaps such delicate reserve about God is no worse than its opposite, or as bad.

Wordsworth was only thirty years of age when he wrote "The Prelude," but he was thoroughly mature as he testified how all the "terrors, pains, and early miseries" had played a necessary part in his development up to his present stage of "calm existence." If Milton rather than Wordsworth had written this poem I think he might have used his own phrase "sober certainty of waking bliss"[4] rather than "calm existence," for that indeed is what such moments bring.

We, too, experience those early and later miseries. Not all of us are given to see them as signs of that *dark inscrutable workmanship* that reconciles discordant elements within us. One must have that faith in God which is faith in life to see them thus. Faith is a gift of God offered to all but received only by some. It is so priceless an asset that why everybody in his right mind does not embrace it I do not know. Only the Inscrutable Workman can have the answer to that.

If we have received the gift of faith and have put it to use, we see that there is sense and purpose in those past afflictions that were so painful to experience and are so painful to recall, even though we do not see specifically *what* that sense and purpose is. Faith does not provide us with such information. Rather, it assures us that there is ultimate sense and purpose in existence itself. Christianity does not tell us why the sparrow falls to the ground; it assures us that it does not fall "without the Father,"[5] and that when the time comes when we shall know even as now we are known[6] we shall then be given the explanation we want—if, then, we shall still want it.

To illustrate how my faith in him whose *dark inscrutable workmanship* in my life makes ever-increasing sense to me, I will now set down a personal experience that is both painful and joyful in the recollection: painful because it began with something long ago that I shall forever wish I could undo, joyful because it is a shining token to me that God not only returns good for my evil but even turns my evil instrumentally into good.

On every Easter Day since I was five years old I have done a penance of memory for what I did on that day. It was a beautiful spring morning. I went out into our backyard and saw a robin resting on our clothesline. I rushed into the house and got a sling-shot, came back and stood under the bird, shot and killed it. As it lay dying at my feet its eyes asked me a question burned forever upon my memory: "Why did you kill me?" From that day to this, over more than sixty years, I have longed for an opportunity to ask the robin's forgiveness. I pray, and I believe, that when I reach the eternal Home of both the robin and me I shall be given that opportunity. I have no doubt that God has forgiven me the sin, but I am equally sure that he does not want me to forget it. A forgiven sin is not a forgotten sin.

My remembrance of my sin has been beneficial in my life. God has used it to create in me an abhorrence of cruelty and of disregard for life in all its forms. I am an active humanitarian, and have been over many years. The seed of this development in my life was sown through my misdeed on that Easter morning in 1917. Of this I am certain. "This is the Lord's doing; it is marvelous in our eyes."[7]

But what of the robin? Did it have to perish so that a cruel little boy should have something to haunt him healthily for the rest of his life? This raises the general question: In God's *dark inscrutable workmanship* is anything being done for the victims of our cruelty or carelessness or ignorance? After all, God is creating not only us but his world as a whole, with everybody and everything in it. Whatever he creates is forever. What, then, of the robin I killed? The circumstances being what they were, I being who I was, it had to die. But it did not have to perish, to be annihilated, to be reduced from something to nothing, and it was not. It did not perish, and never will.

This truth seems to have been intuitively sensed by Israel's great ruler, David the King. He is remembered as "the sweet singer of Israel,"[8] also as an adulterer[9] and a murderer.[10] The child of his adulterous union with Bathsheba was stricken and died. While the child was still living, David fasted and prayed for his recovery. When the child died, David said: "Now that he is dead, wherefore should I fast? Can I bring him back again? I shall go to him, but he shall not return to me."[11] This touching episode moved Lizette Woodworth Reese to write:

> When I consider life and its few years—
> A wisp of fog between us and the sun;
> A call to battle and the battle done
> Ere the last echo dies within our ears;
> A rose choked in the grass; an hour of fears;
> The gusts that past a darkening shore do beat;
> A burst of music down an unlistening street—
> I wonder at the idleness of tears.
> Ye old, old dead, and ye of yesternight,
> Chieftains and bards and keepers of the sheep:
> By every cup of sorrow that you had,
> Loose me from tears, and make me see aright
> How each hath back what once he stayed to weep;
> Homer his sight; David his little lad![12]

Lizette Reese evidently prayed for and believed in what I pray for and believe in: the restoration of all things. In one of the first Christian sermons, St. Peter declared that Christ, having ascended, must remain in heaven "until the times of the restoration of all things of which God has spoken by the mouths of the holy prophets from of old.''[13] The prophets had predicted the restoration to Israel of the old political kingdom of the house of David. But Peter could hardly have meant that, because not many days earlier Jesus had told him and the other disciples expressly that they were to expect something very different from that kind of temporal restoration.[14] Peter meant a restoration universal in scope and eternal in character, even though he may have had no clear idea of what this would consist. Indeed, the meaning of the promise still needs to be spelled out in Christian eschatology, and perhaps that cannot be until the End when we shall see it for ourselves. I venture that it means what the words declare: that all that has been temporally lost is eternally restored; that all that has been sundered is reunited; that to Homer is restored his sight, to Beethoven his hearing, to David his little lad—and to my robin its life and *joie de vivre.*

The Inscrutable Workman is making ingenious use of all these absurdities, cruelties, and injustices to build his new heaven and new earth. Deep in his unfathomable mines with his never-failing skill he is working it all out. He never uses any creature of his love, however insignificant in our sight, simply as a means to an end, to be scrapped as soon as his end has been accomplished. Nothing can be a mere tool, or a mere anything, to God. He created it because he loved it, and his everlasting love will never uncreate any object of it.

In his preface to Dickens's *Pickwick Papers,* Chesterton discusses the nature of creativity in an artist and says: ''The whole difference between construction and creation is exactly this: that a thing constructed can only be loved after it is constructed; but a thing created is loved before it exists.''[15] God loved ''my'' robin into being, and that is why it exists today and forever. If this were not so, it would be because I had the power to uncreate what God had created: *quid est absurdum.* Am I saying that the robin experienced some kind of resurrection from death to life? No, not really. It died temporally but did not perish eternally. I say that it lives because God who loved it into being for his own pleasure cannot be robbed of his treasure by a little boy with a slingshot.

Once it is accepted that nothing whatever exists except that which God creates in love, it becomes inconceivable that any object of God's love can ever be scrapped. God has no cosmic junkyard. Not even hell can be that. If God junked anybody or anything it would have to be either (a) because he had ceased to love it, or (b) because he could no longer use it to his own glory and to its own fulfillment.

By his *dark inscrutable workmanship* in every corner of his creation and in every human self, God is working his sovereign will toward the restoration, in Christ, of all things that need to be restored, and toward the completion of all things that need to be completed if his joy, and creation's joy, is to be made full.

NOTES

1. Matthew Arnold: "The enduring power, not ourselves, which makes for righteousness." *Literature and Dogma,* I, 5.
2. I have forgotten who it was, but I think it was André Maurois.
3. William Wordsworth, "Lines Written in Early Spring."
4. Milton, *Comus,* 263.
5. Matthew 10:29.
6. 1 Corinthians 13:12.
7. Psalm 118:23.
8. 2 Samuel 23:1.
9. 2 Samuel 11:4.
10. 2 Samuel 11:7–17.
11. 2 Samuel 12:23.
12. Lizette Woodworth Reese, *A Wayside Lute,* "Tears."
13. Acts 3:21.
14. Acts 1:7–8.
15. G. K. Chesterton, in the preface to the Everyman's edition of Charles Dickens, *The Pickwick Papers.*

ELEVEN

DEATH THE LUBRICANT

> We must overcome death by finding God in it.
> Teilhard de Chardin, *The Divine Milieu*

Death has been given countless names by mortals, most of them bad ones. I find helpful this comment by Henri de Montherlant: "I can imagine a religion in which death would be represented symbolically as oil, because it is the oil of the machinery of the universe."[1] When you shift the gears of your automobile there is a lubricant that makes it possible. Death lubricates for gear-shifting all forms of life throughout all the machinery of the universe. Your present life comes to you by courtesy of millions of your human forebears and of your prehuman forebears all the way back to Pooh Bah's "protoplasmic primordial atomic globule."[2] They all had to die so that you could be born. If we ourselves are not personally engaged in the procreation of children we are nonetheless consuming oxygen and occupying precious space that must be relinquished to make room for those to come.

I have to say that I find philosophically preposterous, morally offensive, and theologically defamatory of God's good name the hoary doctrine that *physical* death is a punishment that we must suffer for our crime of being descended from our wayward ancestor

Adam. And in no way does the Bible make it obligatory for believ-
ers.

When Jesus (according to St. John) declares that if any man keeps
his saying he shall never taste of death, he is not promising that if
we believe in him we shall never experience bodily death. What a
terrible fate that would be, really! But the *fear and dread* of death is
obviously the punishment that befalls the soul who is alienated from
God. To such a one the death of this mortal body must be, as
Browning calls it in "Prospice," "the Arch Fear in a visible form."
He who "tastes" death tastes the bitterness of parting with that
which he loves more than God—his own life. This is the sting of
death for him who lives unto himself. To live with Christ in God
is to be delivered from that anguish and to be able to say with Paul:
"For me to live is Christ, and to die is gain."

We really need two words for death: one for the death of the
body, the other for the death of the self. The former is an event
functioning as the lubricant of life. The latter is the condition of
having fallen from that life in God which is the only true life.

To love and know God as he reveals himself to us in Christ and
yet to fear the death of the body is entirely illogical. However, the
fact that you may not be impatient to die at this moment is not
evidence in itself that you are afraid to die. This life that God has
given us is good, and if you find it appetizing and delicious it is
both natural and right that you want to keep it until it has lost its
savor. Even when this life is painful or sorrowful it is still a blessed
gift. One day the sons of an old Victorian gentleman, one of Chesterton's grandfathers, were criticizing the General Thanksgiving in
the Book of Common Prayer and remarking that many people have
little cause to thank God for their creation. The old man spoke up
with feeble voice but firm conviction to say "I should thank God
for my creation if I knew I was a lost soul."[3] If any Christian lacks
that gratitude for the simple fact of his existence, the authenticity
of his Christianity is questionable.

Death as a lubricant makes possible the movement of our life to
the next stage of life. It also lubricates our present life from day to

day in a very necessary way, by being another kind of death that keeps us living and growing. We grow by such dying. Lewis Mumford observed in one of his earlier books that "man truly lives by scrapping his old dead selves."[4] Physicians use the term "vital signs" to indicate the physiological evidences of life. This excellent phrase may be applied to spiritual life. The death of your old self at any point in your life is a wonderfully bright vital sign of the new self in you. The old Scrooge died on that glorious Christmas morning, and that death was the best gift the new Scrooge could possibly have received.

Genuine growth within one's self is an unspeakable blessing—and a continuous dying. As Professor A. E. Taylor put it: "Our task as moral beings is to lead a 'dying life'; to rest on our oars would mean a 'living death,' a very different thing."[5]

"We must overcome death by finding God in it," as Father Teilhard reminds us. We could also say that we must overcome death by letting God find us in it. We could also say that we must overcome death by letting God find us in it. Death is a summons. Our Father is calling us to come up higher, in the sense that a soldier comes up higher when he is promoted in rank, given more power, more responsibility. There are some words in a parable of Jesus that represent what I believe to be the substance of what the Lord says to us at our death if we have been faithful: "Well done, good and faithful servant. You have been faithful over a few things, I will make you ruler over many things. Enter now into the joy of your Lord."[6]

We shall find God in our death if now we find him in our life by letting ourselves be found by him. John Greenleaf Whittier, the Quaker poet, lived a life of quiet but active obedience to Christ. Therefore he could testify:

> No offering of my own I have,
> Nor works my faith to prove;
> I can but give the gifts He gave,
> And plead His love for love.

And so beside the Silent Sea
I wait the muffled oar,
No harm from Him can come to me
On ocean or on shore.

I know not where His islands lift
Their fronded palms in air,
I only know, I cannot drift
Beyond His love and care.[7]

Something mysterious happens in the inmost being of the person who lives such an offered life. He does these "few things" that may be mostly little things demanding little, but as he does them there grows in him the feeling that what he is doing is somehow preparatory for more and greater things—where? When? How? He does not know and cannot learn. But this feeling was surely in William James as he remarked on his seventieth birthday that he was just getting fit to live. This feeling makes sense if it be that God is teaching us through it the rudiments of some higher service yet to come. It implies that our present life is an apprenticeship for the Larger Life and the Perfect Service.

Nobody in this world follows the Way of Christ just for the fun of it. There can and ought to be fun and pleasure in it, but being a faithful Christian is not its own reward in the way that being a successful hedonist is. The Christian life points beyond this world for its consummation and fulfillment, and its continuation on a higher plane of being.

Matthew Arnold is not remembered as a man of superabundant faith. In his splendid poetry we often find expressions of a melancholy agnosticism. But one evening in November 1857, he stood in the chapel of Rugby School, whose peerless master his father had been, and he meditated beside his father's tomb. So vivid and powerful had been Thomas Arnold's personality that when his son, and others who had known him, tried to think of him in heaven they could only think of him as they had known him. Yet they thought of him as being now and forever in a dimension of being in which he could be more his true self. Thus his son mused:

> O strong soul, by what shore
> Tarriest thou now? For that force,
> Surely, has not been left vain!
> Somewhere, surely, afar
> In the sounding labor-house vast
> Of being, is practised that strength,
> Zealous, beneficent, firm!
>
> Yes, in some far-shining sphere,
> Conscious or not of the past,
> Still thou performest the word
> Of the Spirit in whom thou dost live—
> Prompt, unwearied, as here!
> Still thou upraisest with zeal
> The humble good from the ground,
> Sternly repressest the bad!
> Still, like a trumpet, dost rouse
> Those who with half-open eyes
> Tread the border-land dim
> 'Twixt vice and virtue; reviv'st,
> Succorest!—this was thy work,
> This was thy life upon earth.[8]

This was his life upon earth. Are we to assume that this is also his life in heaven, in God our Home? Any assumption about that must be speculative, but it need not be wildly and irrationally so if we have in us that feel of eternity that we have earlier considered, the feel that is educated and controlled by the mind of Christ.

Matthew Arnold could see his father in his higher life sternly repressing the bad. He had caned wayward boys while here; is there caning to do "there"? He could see his father zealously lifting the humble good from the ground. He could see him rousing and awakening to better thinking those whose moral perceptions were murky, in heaven as he had done on earth. In such speculation he raises for us this question: Do such particular tasks as have been given us to do on earth, and others like them, remain for us to do in the higher life? If the answer to that question is yes, this one follows: With our present imaginative equipment, how are we to think of the faithful servants of God in heaven actually doing their work? God has made them masters over many things because here they were faithful in few things. Then what are those many things and how are they mastered?

Nothing in the Christian revelation gives us anything like a direct answer to these questions. But this book is an exploration of a passionate intuition, and I boldly avail myself of what I shall call explorer's license. These things I firmly believe:

Death is "the oil of the machinery of the universe." It makes possible God's shifting us from a lower to a higher gear.

Our present life is an apprenticeship for a life infinitely transcending this one in power, goodness, beauty, and joy. I eschew the term "probationary" because of its penal overtones. We are not "on probation" as offenders. God is educating and orienting us now for the fulfillment of our life in eternity.

Matthew Arnold's intuition of his father's life in God was based upon an insight that we may reasonably pursue in our own thinking, but before we can profitably do that we may need to reeducate our minds, more especially our imaginations, as to what heaven as life in God really is. If we restrict our idea of it to some "happy harbor of the saints," a "sweet and pleasant soil" in which "no sorrow may be found, no grief, no care, no toil,"[9] then, of course, it is ridiculous to imagine that in heaven there is anything like bad boys needing to be caned and moral gropers who need somebody like Thomas Arnold to show them the way. But that is a terribly cramped and cramping idea of heaven. We do better to think of heaven as the power-center of the universe. It is headquarters for God and all who serve him day and night in his temple—which is his whole creation. If this little planet, our temporal home, is a fair specimen of the created universe as a whole in its Home in God, there is plenty of good work needing to be done in it by Thomas Arnold and—we may modestly hope and fervently pray—by you and me.

NOTES

1. Henri de Montherlant, "Explicit Mysterium," in *Selected Essays,* (New York: Macmillan, 1961), p. 102.
2. W. S. Gilbert, *The Mikado,* I.
3. G. K. Chesterton, *The Autobiography of G. K. Chesterton* (New York: Sheed and Ward, 1936), p. 12.
4. I cannot remember which one.
5. A. E. Taylor, *The Faith of a Moralist* (London: Macmillan, 1932), vol. 1, p. 132.
6. Matthew 25:14–29. It should be noted that this parable is not about death but about stewardship. I say only that these words of the master in the story strike me as essentially what God has to say to us at the end of our earthly apprenticeship.
7. John Greenleaf Whittier, "The Eternal Goodness."
8. Matthew Arnold, "Rugby Chapel."
9. From the hymn "O Mother Dear, Jerusalem," widely sung throughout Christendom.

TWELVE

RELAXING
ABOUT ANTINOMIES

God is day and night, winter and summer,
war and peace, surfeit and hunger.
— Heraclitus, *Fragments*

How can we think intelligently about our eternal life in God when we can hardly think straight for ten consecutive minutes about our present life amongst the baffling molecules of lowly earth? A nice question; but one which I quit asking myself some years ago for what I hope is a sound reason. The question itself is a statement based upon the premise that it is easier to think about people, chemical elements, calories, and politics than to think about God and the Things Unseen that are ultimate truth. Is not God considerably farther away from us, therefore farther beyond range of our firsthand experience, than is our mother-in-law who has come to live with us?

That question assumes that the answer is, "Yes, of course. Any fool can see that." Any fool can see it, no doubt, precisely because he is a fool; for it isn't true. God is not obvious, but if we think straight we find him considerably less mysterious than any "simple" human fact you can mention. One incontrovertible example from among a million possibilities will make the point. Any American who sees commercial advertisements on television must ask himself: How can the bright people who prepare this often idiotic stuff expect by such absurd tactics to sell the goods to reasonably intelligent viewers like me? The answer to that, alas, is clear enough. These bright people have discovered that intelligent viewers like you and me like to be flimflammed against our own best interest. Simpletons we may be; but how "simple" are we compared to God?

Adlai E. Stevenson once said: "I believe in the forgiveness of sins and the redemption of ignorance." With one addition I make that credo my own: I believe in the simplicity of God, the forgiveness of sins, and the redemption of ignorance. All my ignorance will be transformed into knowledge when I reach Home. It is only temporal and I can live with it, since I must live with a far deadlier affliction, my sins. So much for my ignorance and my sins. What of the first article in my threefold credo, the simplicity of God?

Earlier we spoke[1] of the lady who found St. Thomas Aquinas's treatment of the simplicity of God not nearly simple enough for her. God's simplicity is so simple that it seems to us horrendously complex. It is his uncompoundedness. God's simplicity means that there is in him no mixture of elements such as there is in every one of his creatures. God is literally simpler than the amoeba.

When we talk about the "attributes" of God, such as his power, his love, his wisdom, his beauty, we talk as if these were a multiplicity of qualities in one being; and we are wrong, but it seems that we are wrong by verbal and conceptual necessity. We do this because the only beings we know are multipartite. We know our own selves to be multiple personalities. You know that you are loving, hateful, giving, getting, vain, humble, brave, cowardly, and a thousand other contradictory things all at once. We all are; and we reason that if we are complex God must be more so. It is always bad business reasoning from us to God. It always leads to error. We may, by his grace, grow into likeness to him, but that is precisely because he is *not* like us; and so to try to reason from us to him is like trying to reason from shadow to substance.

All of God's "attributes" are ultimate; none of ours are. If we are right in calling God just it is because he *is* Justice; he *is* Power; he *is* Beauty; he *is* Love. He is the ultimate, and he is also the source of all the things we call by these names. When we speak of a human being as just or powerful or beautiful or loving we are speaking of these qualities in a derivative and limited degree. That is why, for example, we do not see how you or I can be perfectly just and perfectly merciful at the same time. Indeed we cannot. This is because we do not have perfect justice and perfect love, as God has—and is.

Now, as long as we are thoroughly aware of this difference between God and ourselves we can think about his attributes and about ours, which are called by the same names as his, without falling into confusion. But this sense of the difference we must keep strong and straight in mind. If we could see God's attributes as they really are, in their fullness and completeness, we should see that they are all *one and the same:* all of them "simply God." The affirmation that God is One is not simply to say that he is one in number; it is also to say that he is perfectly *simplex in se,* simple, uncompounded, unmixed in himself.

That is his simplicity, and a realization of it is essential to sound thinking about God. The epigraph for this chapter, from the Greek philosopher Heraclitus, declares that God is a complex of what we consider opposites—war and peace, etc. Although this philosophy does not come to us through the Bible, it accords with what the Bible as a whole tells us in a thousand different ways, namely, that *as God appears to us* he *seems* to be many conflicting characters all in one. One moment he seems all mercy, the next moment all merciless justice; one moment love, the next wrath; one moment killing us, the next making us alive. Anybody who has so much as skimmed the Bible and skimmed himself will know what I mean. All this *seeming to us* is that and only that. How God *seems* to us gives us no knowledge of God as he truly is.

The old fable about the six blind men who went to see the elephant is a secular parable of our "seeing" God, our conventional way of investigating him. One man grasped the tail of the beast and pronounced sententiously that the elephant is essentially ropelike.

Another touched the elephant's side and compared the animal to a wall; another grasped the tusk and discovered that the elephant is a gigantic spear; and so on through all six. The result was six different and mutually contradictory elephantologies. By a like groping procedure we arrive at our conflicting theologies. As was said of the blind men in the fable so may it be said of us: Each is partly in the right, and all are in the wrong. So long as we try to discover God by blindly groping speculation we do no better than did those six researchers into the essence of elephantism. Well did Zophar the Naamathite ask poor troubled Job: "Canst thou by searching find out God?"[2] Of course not; but as a race we do not seem to know this well enough to quit trying.

God offers us a live option: a way to him in which "wayfaring men, though fools"[3] need not err. We cannot build a ladder into heaven, but God lets down a ladder to us, as he did to Jacob in his dream,[4] on which the angels of revelation descend and the angels of response ascend. No poet has ever expressed this truth more beautifully than Francis Thompson:

> O world invisible, we view thee,
> O world intangible, we touch thee,
> O world unknowable, we know thee,
> Inapprehensible, we clutch thee!
>
> Does the fish soar to find the ocean,
> The eagle plunge to find the air—
> That we ask of the stars in motion
> If they have rumour of thee there?
>
> Not where the wheeling systems darken,
> And our benumbed conceiving soars!—
> The drift of pinions, would we hearken,
> Beats at our clay-shuttered doors.
>
> The angels keep their ancient places;—
> Turn but a stone, and start a wing!

'Tis ye, 'tis your estrangèd faces,
That miss the many-splendoured thing.

But (when so sad thou canst not sadder)
Cry;—and upon thy so sore loss
Shall shine the traffic of Jacob's ladder
Pitched betwixt Heaven and Charing Cross.

Yea, in the night, my Soul, my daughter,
Cry,—clinging Heaven by the hems;
And lo, Christ walking on the water,
Not of Gennesareth, but Thames![5]

God shows himself to us as fast as we grow up into a capacity to receive his self-revelation with an understanding commensurate to our readiness. To grow in the knowledge and love of Christ is to grow in the vision of God. "He that hath seen me hath seen the Father," Jesus says.[6] We do not see all of God in Jesus, but what we see in Jesus is all God. (It is all man too. There is no contradiction here.) And this vision of the Father that he gives us in his Son is all the vision of God we need to see us all the way Home. Once there, we may begin a whole new stage of education in God, if that is his will and pleasure.

I started this chapter intending to deal with the problem of antinomy in thinking about God. An antinomy in theology is a seeming, apparent contradiction between two affirmations about God. In the last paragraph I stated a familiar Christian antinomy when I said that in Jesus we see a man who is all God and a God who is all man. That is an apparent contradiction. But it appears so to us because we are ignorant of both God and man. Not only do we not know God in his fullness, we do not know ourselves in our fullness. If we were to meet a complete human being on the street I doubt that we should recognize him as "one of us" any more than we should recognize God-in-himself on the street. (Actually, we are meeting God on the street all the time, and we do not recognize him, but because he recognizes us we live.)

Because of our ignorance of God's attributes in their ultimate reality we try vainly to reconcile what we see with what we do not yet see, as when we ask: "How can we reconcile the extermination of six million Jews in the Nazi death camps with God's love and power?" Another ignorance that makes all such efforts at "reconciliation" futile, and even presumptuous, is our ignorance of God's purposes. One of the most tremendous theological statements ever made by anybody outside the Bible was made by Lincoln in his second inaugural address. It is in the little word "own" in this sentence: "The Almighty has his own purposes." That means that they are not *our* purposes, and they do not have to agree with our purposes. God does not announce his plans and purposes at press conferences or otherwise. We don't like this. We would much rather have him clear things with us, but he doesn't.

God's life, unlike ours, has no antinomies in it, but our present concept of God's life and being consists of nothing but antinomies. We can learn to live with them, and when we do we find instant and total relief from that theological *angst*[7] which can murder our sleep. I know; I have found it so in the past, but I no longer waste one moment, which God wants me to spend enjoying him and enjoying being alive, in trying to "reconcile" the divinity of Christ with his humanity or to "reconcile" any other seemingly contradictory elements in the economy of God.

There came a point in my life when I could hear God saying to me something that came through in our primitive tellurian vernacular as this: "I wish you'd leave all this 'reconciling' of things to me, since you are so hopelessly unequipped for it, and that you would use whatever influence you have with your fellow fussers and worriers to persuade them to do likewise. I know what I'm doing. Trust me. I'll go over it all with you when you get Home and clear up any difficulties you have with My managerial procedures. Meanwhile, I want you to find enough loving and enjoying to do during the rest of your days upon earth to keep you both busy and happy."

So I have learned to relax about the antinomies. I hope that what

I have said will help you to do the same, for I am absolutely certain that God wants us to.

We began this chapter with a text from Heraclitus: "God is day and night, winter and summer, war and peace, surfeit and hunger." About a century ago a poet wrote an ode to him which began: "They told me, Heraclitus, they told me you were dead."[8] If I were a poet, I might try a poem beginning:

> *I tell you Heraclitus, I tell you, you were right:*
> *For peace, in God, is war indeed, and day in him is night.*

As you see, I am not a poet.

NOTES

1. At the beginning of chapter seven.
2. Job 11:7.
3. Isaiah 35:18.
4. Genesis 28:10–17; see also John 1:51.
5. Francis Thompson, "In No Strange Land."
6. John 14:9.
7. The German word for "anxiety." It is a blessed word for modern existentialists, none of whom, to the best of my knowledge, can enjoy any peace in this world, not even the peace of God, without feeling guilty.
8. William Johnson Cory, "Heraclitus."

HELL

I ponder "What is Hell?" I maintain it is the
suffering of not being able to love.
　　Fyodor Dostoevsky, *The Brothers Karamazov*

It seems to be very difficult for Christians to think and speak about hell without committing one of two errors. We are tempted to ignore or explain away our Lord's plain warnings of the reality of hell, and in so doing assure ourselves and possibly others that there is really nothing for such enlightened minds as ours to worry about concerning it. (One such theological cavalier told us some years ago that he didn't believe in hell because "we are, literally, not worth a damn" to God.) Or we may be tempted (though this is not nearly so likely today as in former times) to become so morbidly preoccupied with the subject of hell as unending punishment that we lose sight of God's merciful will that not any child of his love should perish, and of his power to bring his own will to pass in all matters.

We find it hard to think in a level-headed and balanced way about hell, both lovingly and seriously, but the effort must be made. If we have a God-given right to think hopefully about heaven we have a God-given duty to think soberly about hell.

One of the appealing things in the writings of Teilhard de Chardin is the way in which he sometimes shifts from exposition of his subject to discursive prayer addressed in print to God. We find ourselves praying along with him as we read; at least I do. In one such prayer, in *The Divine Milieu,* he says:

> You have told me, O God, to believe in hell. But You have forbidden me to hold with absolute certainty that a single man has been damned. I shall therefore make no attempt to consider the damned here, nor even to discover—by whatsoever means— whether there are any. I shall accept the existence of hell on Your word, *as a structural element in the universe,* and I shall pray and meditate until that awe-inspiring thing appears to me as a strengthening and even blessed complement to the vision of Your omnipresence which You have opened out to me.[1]

I find a great and godly wisdom here, or rather, it finds me, and I shall try to follow its light.

Shall we say that hell is "a structural element in the universe"? I don't know what precisely Teilhard had in mind by the phrase, but the American phrase that comes to my mind is "built-in," as in "built-in obsolescence." May it be that what we call "obsolescence" has some relevance to the cosmic reality we are thinking about? Is hell the final state of whoever and whatever obsolesces in this world? I won't pursue that, but it wouldn't make a bad subject for somebody's doctoral dissertation on the subject of what God does with his outworn and outmoded creations.

Certainly, if hell is "a structural element in the universe," God himself has built it in. When the author of the 118th Psalm reflected upon the wonder of how the stone that the builders rejected had been made the cornerstone he exclaimed, "This is the Lord's doing; it is marvelous in our eyes." Hell may be God's rejection of the stones we choose to be our cornerstones, in which case well may we exclaim "This is the Lord's doing, and it is awkward and downright awesome in our eyes."

According to my passionate intuition the whole of creation is in

God: He contains all that he has made, he is contained by nothing. This view is formally called *panentheism,* meaning "all is *in* God," as distinct from *pantheism,* meaning "all *is* God." Please don't call me a pantheist. It is a dirty word for Christians, and I am not guilty. St. Paul in effect declared himself to be a panentheist when he told his audience at Athens that in God "we live and move and have our being."[2] I am in theologically good company with him. All that God ever made is in God, and God made hell as a part of the structure of his universe. I know that this is a most unconventional view of the matter, but I cannot believe that it is original with me: I just don't know who else has said it. It's the way I see it; *Ich kann nicht anders, Gott helfe mir!*

Hell is indeed an awe-inspiring theme, if we stand in awe of God himself. (And if we do not, we are self-disqualified to speak of him.) Kant said that there were two things that filled him with awe: the starry sky above and the moral law within.[3] He would probably have agreed that there is no better verbal formulation of the moral law than the statement that what a man sows that shall he reap.[4] Nobody with eyes to see and a mind to understand can observe without awe the ineluctable working of that law. And that is what makes hell an awe-inspiring theme. If there is no way—and there appears to be none—of anybody's escaping the consequences of defying that law, it follows that there is "hell to pay." Hell is the reaping of whatever evil one has sown. The harvest may come "here" or "hereafter" or both, but come it surely will if the moral law as we have stated it is one of the conditions of our very existence.

What Teilhard said in his prayer about hell is exactly what my heart says: I shall pray and meditate upon it until it appears to me as a strengthening and even blessed complement to the vision of his omnipresence that God has opened out to me. This is to say that I don't yet see, existentially see, what I know that I shall see when I have grown up into that vision: that hell is one more expression of God's love for all his creatures, including those in hell.

I have said that hell is the harvest of whatever evil seed one has sown. But if I were pressed to give a definition of the *character* or nature of hell I would make my own the words of Father Zossima in *The Brothers Karamazov:* "Hell is the suffering of not being able to love."[5] This inability constitutes alienation and separation from God because the only communion with God is participation in God's own life by loving as he loves and loving whomever and whatever he loves (which of course is everybody and everything). That communion is heaven. Lack of it is hell. Those who *live* in God by sharing his loving are in heaven: or, if you prefer, heaven is in them. I have seen a statement attributed to Thomas Hardy to the effect that the object of true religion is not to get a man into heaven but to get heaven into the man. I heartily subscribe, with the proviso that the latter effort is not a logical preclusion of the former. Those who *exist* in God without that participation in the divine life which is God's love *(agape)* are in hell, irrespective of whether they are presently in the flesh or beyond it. And I will add to what Hardy said that the aim of true religion is not to keep a man out of hell but to get hell out of him.

Many modern Christians who abhor the dreadful old conception of hell as a torture chamber have sought an acceptable alternative in the idea that hell may be simply the annihilation of those souls whose rejection of God results at last in his final rejection of them. On that premise, God disposes of them in the way that you dispose of rubbish—he simply trashes them. Thus hell becomes the cosmic junkyard. This may be morally tolerable, at least to them; but to any believer in God's sovereign mastery of his own creation it is theologically unacceptable. If God creates anybody intended for eternal life and that creature ends up in eternal death, God is not sovereign.

Those who will not be God's sons must become his tools. The Assyrian of Isaiah's day was not God's son but God's tool. Where do we go from there—if anywhere? That is not the right question, which is rather: Where does God go from there with the Assyrian? I will confess that I have not spent the past half-hour on the phone with God, getting a briefing upon developments in the case of the recalcitrant or penitent Assyrian. I have no information that you don't have. Moreover, we are not morally obligated to concern ourselves with the case at all: It is outside our moral jurisdiction as well as our juridical. God will not be put out with us if we just leave the Assyrian, and Hitler, and Stalin, and all other such hard cases to him: " 'Vengeance is *mine, I* will repay!' saith the Lord."[6]

But I cannot leave it alone. Earlier in this book I reported my annual Easter penance for the murder of the robin. I hope it doesn't sound ridiculous to you, for it certainly isn't to me, when I say that I cannot regard the Assyrian as being somehow *categorically* different from me, or me from him. "There but for the grace of God go I." In saying that, I am not being charitable, only realistic. The robin episode is not the only evidence known to God, and even to myself, that I have been guilty of finding pleasure in destroying the works and creatures of God's love, as did the Assyrian, only on a different scale. He grew up and lived out his days in a moral and spiritual environment far different from mine, and vastly inferior. So I (and perhaps you) have a proper personal interest in the case of the Assyrian. His is a kind of class-action case, because there is an Assyrian in every one of us and he sometimes breaks loose.

We who constitute this common class, the human race, are created in God's image. We defile that image by our ungodliness, which means ungodlikeness, and we die in our sins. There is no human being who does not belong to this class. And so God's problem, his unfinished business, with us both now and at our death is the same with us all. We, like the Assyrian, need to be not merely retreaded but rebuilt: though not totally replaced.

The above is a metaphor borrowed from the business of automobile tires. I don't think it's too bad, but you may prefer, as in fact I do, the more familiar metaphor in which our earthly life is seen as our elementary education for an eternal future. Robert Frost said in one of his most familiar lines: "Earth's the right place for love: I don't know where it's likely to go better."[7] Earth is the place where we must learn to love; that's what our existence is all about. We all finish this terrestrial schooling short of a perfect record, but some of us do better than others—or fondly fancy that we do, and so we get to grading ourselves and our fellow learners. St. Francis and Mother Teresa and Florence Nightingale and some others carry off top honors with no grade lower than an A-minus. Judas, Stalin, King Lear's evil daughters, the man in our neighborhood who puts out poison for dogs, get nothing better than an F from us, a flat flunk. To hell with them!

How do we grade ourselves? At Harvard there's something called a Gentleman's C. We know that we are not exactly top-grade people, and claiming just a C for ourselves must impress God, as it does us, with our becoming modesty. But we do pass. The F is for those who are what we are not and are not what we are.

This can be a pleasant exercise in self-grading and other-grading. But we must understand that it is only a game, and a make-believe game at that. Only God does the real grading: only he *can*. All that we know about God's grading is that it is done with infinite discrimination and divine impartiality to this whole class of which the Assyrian and St. Stephen the Martyr and you and I are all members—all standing in need of prayer. We all die in the condition of not yet being "made perfect in love."[8]

That is what God is confronted with in the Assyrian, and in us.

NOTES

1. Pierre Teilhard de Chardin, *The Divine Milieu,* p. 129.
2. Acts 17:28.
3. Immanuel Kant, *Critique of Pure Reason,* conclusion.
4. Galatians 6:7.
5. Fyodor Dostoevsky, *The Brothers Karamazov,* trans. Constance Garnett (New York: Random House, The Modern Library, 1943) II, vi, 3.
6. Romans 12:19.
7. Robert Frost, "Birches."
8. 1 John 4:18.

PURGATORY

Our souls *demand* Purgatory, don't they? Would it not break the heart if God said to us, "It is true, my son, that your breath smells and your rags drip with mud and slime, but we are charitable here and no one will upbraid you with these things, nor draw away from you. Enter into the joy"? Should we not reply, "With submission, Sir, and if there is no objection, I'd *rather* be cleansed first." "It may hurt, you know." "Even so, Sir."
C. S. Lewis, *Letters to Malcolm: Chiefly on Prayer*

The word "purgatory" sounds dreadful, worse than hell. It sounds too grim for what it is meant to identify, but its only single-word synonym, paradise, seems too rose-gardenish. It may help us to think less apprehensively about purgatory if we reflect that it might well have been called crematory and it wasn't. In Latin a *purgatorium* is a place of cleansing and a *crematorium* is a place where corpses and other rubbish are burnt.

If you have ever visited a mosque you know that all who enter are expected to take off their shoes before coming in, so that they will not bring into God's house the dirt of the sinful world outside. That expresses the instinct which, Lewis says, demands purgatory.

There is nothing new that I can say about the purgatorial expe-

rience, but I believe that our central theme in this book can illumi-
nate it. If, as I contend, all of creation, all of life, all of things past,
present, and to come, is *in God,* then hell is in God and purgatory
is in God no less than heaven. If for us the prospect of purgatory
beyond the grave as well as on this side is a prospect in God, it must
lose its terror. Whatever purgatory is, being in God it is ''owned
and operated'' by the God and Father of Jesus Christ.

> Whither shall I go from thy spirit?
> or whither shall I flee from thy presence?
> If I ascend up into heaven, thou art there:
> if I make my bed in hell, behold, thou art there.
> If I take the wings of the morning,
> and dwell in the uttermost parts of the sea,
> even there shall thy hand lead me,
> and thy right hand shall hold me.
> If I say, surely the darkness shall cover me,
> even the night shall be light about me.
> Yea, the darkness hideth not from thee;
> but the night shineth as the day:
> the darkness and the light are both alike to thee.[1]

The Hebrew poet here declares a truth that, if we let it possess
us, will rid our minds of all fear of death, judgment, hell, and
purgatory. The darkness that covers us in death in God's darkness,
and so it is light. There is no darkness in God's world that is not
in anticipation and preparation for the coming light. This is true in
this present life and in the life to come, and so it is true of the
preparatory and purifying experience we call purgatory.

My own thinking about the Last Things has recently been much
clarified by Peter J. Kreeft, who to my knowledge is the best writer
on this subject since C. S. Lewis. Here are a few illuminating quotes
from his book *Everything You Ever Wanted to Know About Heaven
... But Never Dreamed of Asking:*[2]

1) ''If the word [purgatory] offends you, call it 'Heaven's Kindergarten' instead.''[3]

2) "Purgatory is necessary not only from our point of view but from God's point of view. God wastes nothing. Everything must be completed, must 'come true.' The divine masterpieces that are human selves must ring true; the story that is my life must have its perfect consummation. Our earthly lives are fallow fields, unread books, unmilked cows. All their seeds must flower, all their lessons be learned, all their meanings milked. God's word uttered immediately after Creation must be uttered also at the end: 'Very good.' "[4]

3) "Purgatory is like an incubator. A premature baby is put into an incubator to finish outside the womb the growing that should have been done in the womb. At death our fetal souls are born into heaven in an immature state. Before they are strong enough to survive the heavenly light, they need a 'thickening process.' We now have a baby spirit in an adult body; the spiritual maturity that so lags behind our physical maturity needs a 'physic,' a vitamin, a course in Remedial Spirituality before it can assume the resurrection body, as a child needs lessons in horsemanship using ponies before being able to ride a great and powerful stallion."[5]

The doctrine of purgatory is sometimes regarded as a doctrine of a second chance. About this we need to watch our thoughts and our words most carefully, lest a kindly and optimistic sentimentality beguile us into muddleheadedness. There is absolutely no support in holy scripture or in sound theology for belief in a "second chance," *if*—and here I beg to be read as carefully as I am writing—*if by that term is meant a God-given opportunity to do something over again that was not done right the first time.*

Somebody once lamented, "If my life could have a second edition, how I would revise the text!" I'm sure we all know that feeling. We can't revise the text; but we can go on to revise our living in a way that will bring us through shame and failure to glory and victory.

A dear and thoughtful friend has raised with me this question: "What about Charles Colson of the Watergate scandal? Personally, I think God has given him a 'second chance' here and now on this little planet." I joyfully agree with her about God and Mr. Colson, but what God has given him is not a second chance but really a first one. Mr. Colson is like every one of the rest of us: His life continues in its first and only edition, and because he is enlisted with God he need not revise the text as written in the past but rather to complete the text in the present and future.

What would a second chance consist of, in fact? Imagine a pitcher in the deciding game of the World Series, on a rueful morning after, reflecting upon the pitch he threw to the batter who hit it out of the park to win the game: "If only I had that pitch back! This time I'd throw a sinker low and inside rather than a fast ball high and over the outside of the plate." But he's crying over spilt milk, as are all our lamentations over past mistakes. If he is a Christian he believes in the forgiveness of sins, the unrevisability of the text, and the gracious will of God to make of him a winner in a game infinitely more important even than the last game in the World Series.

God always offers us something far better than any second chance could ever be: a chance to enter what the old Yankee broadcaster Mel Allen called "a brand new ball game."

"To every thing there is a season, and a time for every purpose under the heaven."[6] Just one season, just one time, just one moment. Perhaps God put it into my mind yesterday to go to visit a lonely old soul in a nursing home, and I didn't. That was my only chance to do it when he wanted me to do it. I may make that visit today, but that is not a second chance to do what could only be done yesterday, when God asked me to do it. There is never a second chance about anything for anybody, either here and now or there and thereafter. This truth we need both to forget and to remember: to quit crying about it and to start doing the things God gives us to do at the times when he gives them to us to do.

There may be in purgatory or paradise a *first* chance for the Assyrian, or for Dismas, or for our own selves. We, too may properly be called deprived persons (no offense intended). Some things that we might regard as spiritual assets can work in us as liabilities because we misuse them. You might, for example, be the child of spiritually mature parents who have given you the best kind of upbringing—with the result that you became a holier-than-thou prig of the worst sort. In our own ways we are all deprived, by our own fault or otherwise. Purgatory, in whatever form it comes to us either here or hereafter, may provide for us a first chance to come into our own as children of God. That is the divine end and purpose of it. We hope that when we depart this life we shall do so with our sins forgiven, but even if we do we shall be dragging with us the memory of a long and sorry list of first-and-only chances that were missed or misused. Thank God there is Somebody Over There who can take hold of us poor losers and make winners of us—if that's what we want.

In any consideration of eternal life we need to give a thought to reincarnation. Many people, Christians among them, are attracted to the idea of reincarnation because of their longing for a second chance to redo some, many, or all past events in their lives. They feel they could best do this if one day they could return to this earth as somebody who is yet unborn. I have often been asked if, in my opinion, reincarnation is compatible with Christian belief. Quite evidently the number of Christians who ask this question is growing.

I can only reply that reincarnation, as I see it, is incompatible with belief in the resurrection of the body and the life everlasting. Jews and Christians whose faith is rooted in the self-disclosure of the living God, which is the whole theme of the Bible, believe in a God who leads his people, and his whole creation, onward from one stage to the next, from age to age. History never repeats itself. The eternally living and working God[7] is constantly making all things new: *all* things.[8] The "second chance" that a reincarnation would presumably make possible is alien to God's way of continuing his creation.

To people who believe in, or long for, that chance to relive their lives here on earth may reasonably be put this question: What makes you think you would do better the second time around? If they answer that they are wiser now as a result of learning from their mistakes, we should have to remind them that if God were to give them a real second chance he would have to roll back not only the calendar but their own lives to the exact point at which they got their lifelong series of first chances. And we might ask them this question also: If it is God's will that we be given such "second chances" in some later incarnate existence on earth, to redeem our failures and misdeeds in our past, why do not all of us have some clear recollection of our sins and mistakes in our previous incarnations so that we can redeem them now?

Reincarnation is really a metaphysical concept rather than a religious one (which is not to say that it is antireligious). An atheist can believe wholeheartedly in reincarnation, and in fact some do. Only one whose faith is rooted in the biblical tradition, who is entirely certain that God is constantly making a new being out of his old being, is prevented by his own theological premises from believing in reincarnation.

Purgatory is the experience in which the Lord takes us as we are and proceeds to cleanse us with healing but astringent waters. If I am asked how I think I can know anything at all about purgatory before I have died, I answer that what I know, or think that I know, about purgatory consists entirely of what I experience of it in my present life. The God with whom I have to deal now is the God with whom I shall have to deal then. Purgatory "there," if such there be, will be essentially the same divine healing and creating action that it is here.

But is it a biblical belief? There is no mention of purgatory in the Bible, whereas there are innumerable mentions of heaven and hell. The word as we have it is not mentioned. But I could cite a hundred or so cases in the Bible in which it is declared that God took hold of a sinner or scoundrel or fool and made of him or her a servant-child after God's own heart. Purgatory is the cleansing and completion of a defiled and infantile soul who longs to be made fit and ready for eternal life in God our Home. If you believe that God really does that for those who want it, you believe in purgatory. But if for whatever reason you don't like the word, as Peter Kreeft suggests, call it "heaven's kindergarten" instead.

One of Oscar Wilde's characters says: "The only difference between a saint and a sinner is that every saint has a past, and every sinner has a future."[9] The truth in that statement is the truth of purgatory.

NOTES

1. Psalm 139:7–12.
2. Peter J. Kreeft, *Everything You Ever Wanted to Know About Heaven . . . But Never Dreamed of Asking* (New York: Harper & Row, Publishers, 1982).
3. Ibid., p. 22.
4. Ibid.
5. Ibid.
6. Ecclesiastes 3:1.
7. John 5:17.
8. Revelation 21:5.
9. Oscar Wilde, *A Woman of No Importance,* III.

FIFTEEN

GOD'S GOOD-FOR-NOTHINGS

God and Nature do nothing uselessly.
Aristotle, *On the Heavens*

Increasingly over the years I have come to believe that the supreme work of Christ, "through whom all things were made,"[1] is to make all creatures useful and delightful to the Father. *All* creatures. That includes all those of our human kind whom we call ne'er-do-wells and good-for-nothings. How can anybody read the Gospels and fail to see how Jesus, in his contacts with all sorts and conditions of people, even the apparent good-for-nothings and worse, always seemed to find in them possibilities for sublime development?

Our judgment upon such human "trash" may be uncharitable but it may not be unrealistic, at least from our extremely limited and myopic point of view. If we do not see how they can possibly be of any use to us we find it even more inconceivable that they can be of any use to God or of any pleasure to him. How can he possibly use them as good instruments in his continuing work of creation?

And, as it seems to us, if that is true of many human beings, how much more true must it be of the constant swarms of animal and vegetable pests that infest our planet? (Note how easily I said "our" planet and how easily you let me go uncorrected! Here is a clue to our almost total lack of comprehension. We think this is our planet rather than God's.)

Christ is working with us now, trying to make us people more useful to God both here and hereafter. In ways unknown to us he is working with all of God's creatures toward the same end, including those we call our natural enemies: the malaria mosquito, poison ivy, et al. He is shepherding and animating the world from within, preparing it for the New Creation as he has been doing from the beginning. If this planet is here a hundred years from now, or a million, it will be a very different place from what it is at this moment because he will have been working with it toward that divine Event to which the whole creation moves.

How, then, can we form some conception, if any, of the way in which God eternally uses all people as agents, and all things as instruments, in his continuing creation, especially those that seem to us worthless, useless, or worse?

As we think into the question we should remind ourselves, first, that a person or thing that seems useless to us may be extremely useful to God. The fact that we do not see how it can be so in no way alters the case. Let us imagine a retarded person in a hospital, whose mental capacity is extremely limited but who loves God and all of God's creatures with that purity of heart and intensity of will that is so often found in those whom we call handicapped. This person prays constantly for everybody in his life. It is all he can do. But in so doing he may "labor more abundantly than they all"[2] for others who suppose that they are caring for him rather than he for them. God can, if he chooses, give *us* "custodial care" through such ministers of his providence. After all, the fact that we cannot see him doing so is entirely irrelevant. We can never see God's caring for us through any of his agents and instruments: not as that caring really is. All of the essential functioning of God's providence is both invisible and incomprehensible to us; but if we have any firsthand knowledge of God, we have learned enough of his inscrutability to realize that we "can't put it past him" to care for us most of all through people whom we consider dependent upon us. We cannot possibly know who are our best friends in this world, if by friends we mean those who do the most as agents of God's care for us. I am sure that this is one of those things that will have our eyes fairly popping out on that day when the secrets of all lives shall be disclosed.

"Be not forgetful to entertain strangers: for thereby some have entertained angels unawares."[3] Behind this lovely New Testament text lies the Old Testament story (Genesis 18) of how three men came to the tent of Abraham and Sarah. To all appearances they were desert hobos, footsore, dirty, hungry and thirsty. But they were given kind hospitality and they brought to the couple the message from God that they would be given a son in their old age. These visitors were shabby men, not gods or heroes; but they were also angels, for they were messengers from God and that is what angels are by proper definition. The dog that brings rescue to a man lost in snow is an angel no less than Raphael or Gabriel. Gungha Din, "for all 'is dirty 'ide," was an angel to the British soldiers under fire. It is God himself who comes to us in his angels, whoever or whatever they may be. The Most High regularly assumes the character of the Most Low in his ministering to us; and only as we see this, and we recognize, welcome, and adore God in his lowliest and "littlest" angels, can we begin to understand how he actively rules and builds his creation. God has no pride. We are given a vision of this great and mighty wonder when we see his divine Son, "the express image of his person,"[4] girding himself with a towel and washing his disciples' feet.[5]

Coleridge said that "Prayer is the effort to live in the spirit of the whole."[6] I will not say that the whole of Christian prayer is in that definition, but I will say that prayer which lacks that effort falls short of being Christian. The whole of God's creation is so much vaster than our fathers dreamt of and than we can dream of! The awareness of this has led me to a strong conviction that God uses us eternally in manifold tasks beyond our present imagining, in tasks not only on this planet but on other planets and in other parts of his immense and ever-growing universe. When Jesus said "the field is the world"[7] he may well have had in mind a much bigger field than this tiny planet in a minor solar system. My very amateurish reading of astronomy has combined with my reading of the following poem by Alice Meynell to create and confirm in me this conviction.

> *With this ambiguous earth*
> *His dealings have been told us. These abide:*
> *The signal to a maid, the human birth,*
> *The lesson, and the young Man crucified.*
>
> *But not a star of all*
> *The innumerable host of stars has heard*
> *How he administered this terrestrial ball.*
> *Our race have kept their Lord's entrusted Word....*
>
> *No planet knows that this*
> *Our wayside planet, carrying land and wave,*
> *Love and life multiplied, and pain and bliss,*
> *Bears, as chief treasure, one forsaken grave.*
>
> *Nor, in our little day,*
> *May his devices with the heavens be guessed,*
> *His pilgrimage to thread the Milky Way,*
> *Or his bestowals there be manifest.*
>
> *But, in the eternities,*
> *Doubtless we shall compare together, hear*
> *A million alien Gospels, in what guise*
> *He trod the Pleiades, the Lyre, the Bear.*
>
> *O be prepared, my soul!*
> *To read the inconceivable, to scan*
> *The million forms of God those stars unroll*
> *When, in our turn, we show to them a Man.*[8]

Meynell was a most orthodox Christian and she is not suggesting a million Christs for a million stars. There is only one Word of the

Father, through whom all things throughout all creation are made and ruled, by whom all things consist.[9] Christ the Word may, however, have a million ways of dealing with a million stars. Alice Meynell had no doubt of that, and neither have I.

At the end of chapter one, we considered the implication of Christ's promise that he will lead us "into all truth."[10] This means that truth is literally boundless and bottomless, an infinite realm that can be familiar terrain only to God. Christ can be leading us into it forever and ever.

With that in mind, we need to consider another promise of Christ recorded by St. John, this one in words beautiful and beloved by all who know them in the King James Version: "In my Father's house are many mansions. . . . I go to prepare a place for you."[11] Quite obviously "mansions" here do not mean what they mean in our contemporary idiom, viz., palatial domiciles fit for kings or for major stockholders of multibillion-dollar corporations. The Greek word translated "mansions" means primarily abiding-places, with no reference to their size or grandiosity. But in late Greek, such as St. John's, the word came to mean "station." Along the caravan trails of that world were way stations for travelers. These were watering places for man and beast, safe and sheltered camp sites for the night.

The beloved text may be legitimately understood as saying to us: In my Father's house, which is this whole universe, there are many resting places along the way on which I am leading you, and I am going on ahead to prepare them for you.

In Thackeray's novel *The Newcomes* a kind old gentleman named James Binnie dies. On his deathbed he is visited by a stern divine, the Reverend Dr. M'Graw, who could never forgive the deceased for not having taken more seriously the Reverend Doctor's literally dread-full sermons. He expressed his firm conviction that the offender was now being punished for his transgression. Thackeray, as was his wont, offered a reflection upon the matter that I find a cogent comment on the "many mansions." He wrote:

Let us hope that the reverend gentleman was mistaken in his views respecting the present position of Mr. James Binnie's soul; and that Heaven may have some regions yet accessible to James, which Dr. M'Graw's intellect has not yet explored. Look, gentlemen! Does a week pass without the announcement of the discovery of a new comet in the sky, a new star in the heaven, twinkling dimly out of a yet farther distance, and only now becoming visible to human ken though existent forever and ever? So let us hope divine truths may be shining, and regions of light and love extant, which Geneva glasses cannot yet perceive, and are beyond the focus of Roman telescopes.[12]

Amen, so might it be. And so, I doubt not, it is.

The metaphor of the way station along the road on which Christ leads us eternally suggests two meanings. These are too often set over against each other in our thinking about the life to come, but they must be held together. It is the kind of antinomy we were thinking about in chapter twelve. Is heaven a realm of rest and peace or a realm of continuing work and service? An either-or answer can only be a half-truth at best, and a half-truth is at best a half-falsehood. The answer must be both-and.

We come to one of these resting places along our way that the Lord has prepared for us, and there is the rest of enjoyment and repose. God's people enjoy this rest on earth in the midst of their pilgrimage. About our rest at last, in God our Home, I know of no wiser and more satisfying words ever spoken than those of Frederick W. Robertson that are quoted in the prologue to this book. Turn to it now and read them thoughtfully. In God our Home we have both perfect rest and perfect service, in that ineffable blending that Robertson describes as well as any mortal can.

Renan said: "Immortality is to labor at an eternal task."[13] That is half of the truth. The other half is music and feasting, love and laughter, in "bliss beyond compare."[14]

For those of us who were considered upon earth (by our fellow human beings and therefore probably by ourselves) to have been not very useful to God or man at our best, and quite good-for-nothing at our worst, perhaps the greatest joy will be to discover that we have been far more useful to God than we have realized, and that our usefulness to him is only beginning after our earthly apprenticeship is ended. We may not have more worlds to conquer, and we did not conquer this one; but God has more worlds than we ever knew existed in which we can serve him, glorify him, and "enjoy him forever."[15]

NOTES

1. John 1:3.
2. 1 Corinthians 15:10.
3. Hebrews 13:2.
4. Hebrews 1:3.
5. John 13:1–17.
6. Coleridge said this some time and somewhere in his "table talk."
7. Matthew 13:38.
8. Alice Meynell, "Christ in the Universe."
9. Colossians 1:17.
10. John 16:13.
11. John 14:2.
12. Henry Makepeace Thackeray, *The Newcomes,* ch. LXV.
13. Ernest Renan, *L'Avenir de la Science,* preface.
14. From the hymn commonly known as "Jerusalem the Golden," originally composed by St. Bernard of Cluny in the twelfth century and translated by John Mason Neale in the nineteenth.
15. "Man's chief end is to glorify God and to enjoy Him forever." *The Westminster Shorter Catechism,* 1647.

SIXTEEN

RESURRECTION

The body of Benjamin Franklin, printer, (like the cover of an old book, its contents torn out and stript of its lettering and gilding,) lies here, food for worms; but the work shall not be lost, for it will (as he believed) appear once more in a new and more elegant edition, revised and corrected by the Author.

Benjamin Franklin, his own epitaph, written at age 22

Somebody has said that Christianity begins where religion ends—with the Resurrection. Of course, everybody has his own way of defining both religion and Christianity, and I have no desire to impose my definitions upon anybody else. I will only say that I accept and make my own the anonymous statement I have just quoted. Before Christ rose from the dead there was much religion in the world; some would say too much for the world's own good, since so much religion has always been thoroughly bad for the human soul. In our time Paul Tillich has defined religion as man's ultimate concern. This definition is widely accepted, and it will do as well as any. For the Christian, ultimate concern becomes ultimate fulfillment when he is raised in Christ from living death to dying life. Thus religion ends and Christianity begins with the Resurrection of Christ, which makes possible our resurrection, in him, from mere existence to new being. Because he lives, we live also.[1]

The Christian belief is in the resurrection of the body, as distinct from the immortality of the soul; but we may have to do some semantic wrestling with the word "body." As I have said earlier,[2] I prefer the word "self" to "soul," and I can almost, though not quite, equate "body" with "self." In ordinary discourse, "body" means the physical organism. When we read that the body of the victim was found in a ditch we know that what is meant is a corpse. Actually, a corpse is an ex-body. Somebody has given up this rather startling and very accurate definition: The body is the socket of the soul. Body is the indispensable integument and also the transmitter of soul. It both sets soul apart from its environment and provides an instrumentality through which soul can connect with other souls and relate to things outside itself. In whatever realm soul lives, whether earth, heaven, paradise, or hell, it must have a body through which to express itself.

The body of the risen Christ, as seen in the New Testament Resurrection narratives, is both a promissory pledge and a type of the bodies with which we begin to be clothed the moment we enter the new life in Christ—as we "put him on."[3] I call Christ's risen body a type: not an exact pattern or blueprint, because the significance of his Resurrection is unique in a sense that our resurrection is not. His is the birth of the New Creation. This being so, it was necessary to God's purpose that when he raised from death to life the Word-made-flesh, this stupendous event should be a visible sign to his chosen witnesses that the old world was dead and the new world had arrived. If those incredulous witnesses were truly to get the message that Death, as power to destroy, had been slain on Calvary by the Lord of life, it was imperative that Christ's bodily appearance to them should be indisputably evident. His death and Resurrection (these must be seen as a single mighty act of God) established the New Creation; our death and resurrection (also a single event) takes place in what he established. And so for God's purpose, and for our own benefit, we do not need to be raised physically and materially from our graves, as was he who is not only "the image of the invisible God" but "the first-born of every creature."[4]

In an excellent modern study of the theology of Resurrection Walter Künneth writes: "The Risen One appears in the glorified form of an inconceivable corporeality, in which a new and wholly other reality is proleptically revealed."[5] Our resurrection-body will share with Christ's that "inconceivable corporeality' even though, unlike his, it may not be given to us while we are still on earth.

We have now a body that will one day become a corpse. Then it will not be a body any longer. Leaving it, we shall enter a realm in which we shall need a new body for our new situation, and we shall be given one. That body will be the plant of which our present body is the seed. More specifically, the seed of that immortal plant which is yet to appear "above ground" is our present self in its physical being. There will be organic continuity between seed and plant such as there is between carrot seed and carrot. The carrot seed exists so that one day it may become a carrot, and that is the truth in the saying of St. Francis de Sales that the world is peopled in order to people heaven. The carrot is the seed come to fruition. Thus is it with human resurrection into fruition, fullness, completion. When our resurrection is complete, we shall be our eternal selves who existed as preselves before our birth, became selves at birth, and through the gate of death entered self-fruition.

I am convinced that when we meet in our eternal bodies we shall greet each other in some such way as this: "I'd know you anywhere, and you look perfectly wonderful; but merciful heaven, how you've changed!" If you and I had been carrot seeds in a package the last time we met, and then months later we met as carrots, might we not say something like that, in whatever language ex-carrot seeds speak as full-blown carrots? "We are the same little precarrot dummies that we were before; but merciful heaven (by the mercy of heaven) how we've changed! Now, having truly come into our own, we are appreciated by discriminating human vegetarians, by all rabbits and all donkeys: rather an exalted end for us originally poor, skinny, insignificant little critters.''

I am suggesting that in our present form and mode we are poor, skinny, insignificant little critters compared to what we shall be in the End, if we live and die in Christ. God is making a beginning with us, and only God knows what he will do when he starts something.

Christianity does indeed begin where religion ends, with the Resurrection, but the whole truth is more wonderful even than that. Our full life begins with our resurrection in Christ, and our resurrection begins when our conversion begins. As Benjamin Whichcote, one of the "Cambridge Platonists" of the seventeenth century, put it: "Entrance into heaven is not at the hour of death, but at the moment of conversion." We must not suppose, however, that "conversion" is all done in a temporal moment. We may be converted *to* Christ in the twinkling of an eye, but conversion *into* Christ must be a lifelong process of the working of grace. The present point, however, is that this is "entrance into heaven," the beginning of our resurrection.

Earlier in this chapter I quoted from Paul's Letter to the Colossians the reference to Christ as "the image of the invisible God" and "the first-born of every creature." The word "creature" *(ktisis)* means not people as such, but all things, everything that God has made, and there is nothing that he has not made. The Resurrection of Christ inaugurates a new order in which every human self, every living creature, every existing thing is brought to its true being by the Power that raised Jesus from the grave.

The first Christians, who suffered so terribly for their faith, felt triumphantly that they were already living in a wonderful new world that was in its travail of birth. Their sufferings were a part of that travail and seemed to them a "light affliction which is but for a moment."[6] That sense of the glorious divine revolution in which every creature is being delivered from "the reign of Chaos and Old Night"[7] into "the glorious liberty of the children of God"[8] is so integral to the Gospel that it is fairly questionable whether our

Christian faith is authentic if we lack it. Christ died and rose again to redeem and perfect all creatures, not just his human elect.

In the most famous of Homer's similes the peerless poet compares the generations of men to the generations of leaves.[9] Christians should prefer to compare man with the tree rather than with the leaf, but even that simile is defective because a tree is no less mortal than its leaves: It takes only a century or so, or perhaps as with some of the more durable a millennium or so, to die, instead of a summer.

We are like a tree in that we die a little with every falling leaf of ours. The leaves we shed are all the dear earthly things, all human friendships, which in their seasons adorned and beautified our lives. Have you ever felt a tinge of sadness when you had to discard an outworn jacket or a pair of shoes that had become somehow a part of you? Our attachment to such things, to say nothing of people, pets, places, routines, pleasures, even dull jobs, can be very deep. God in his love gave them all to us, but he has ordained a time to say good-bye to every one of them. This is among those *lacrimae rerum,* "tears of things," of which Vergil speaks.[10]

But Vergil, like Homer, is pre-Christian. In the light of our res-urrection-faith we may say that the good-bye we must speak to each mortal thing is in fact *au revoir.* When I was a child of four I received a toy train at Christmas. Several months later, after it had been broken and almost forgotten, I asked my mother what had become of it and was told that it had "gone up the spout." I understood that it was kaput. I was satisfied; I would never see it again, and I was not heartbroken. Now I am not so sure that I shall never see it again. Because that toy train once existed, it still exists in some kind of eternal storage. It may even be marked "Hold for C.E.S." All the dogs and cats I have loved long since I have lost only for a while, for if any creature ever exists in God it cannot pass from being into nonbeing.

In St. John's account of the feeding of the five thousand, Jesus instructs his disciples to "gather up the fragments that remain, that nothing be lost."[11] In an earlier chapter[12] we considered the universal and eternal implications of "the restoration of all things."[13] Christ is the eternal gatherer and restorer of all the lost fragments of creation.

That nothing be lost: nothing; nobody; those Victor Red Seal records of Caruso and Galli-Curci for our old windup phonograph; my third-grade teacher who died in the terrible flu epidemic of 1919; all people, all things that ever were. Like leaves they fall to the ground and die. Or may it not be rather that "in the sight of the unwise they *seemed* to die"?[14] What does God do with all these fragments of things he made and of life he gave? God has taught us (me, at least, and undoubtedly some others) through the profoundly Christian mind and pen of George Macdonald that the miracles of Jesus in his incarnate life were signs, made visible to human eyes, of what God is doing eternally and universally.[15] God is gathering up all the fragments of everybody and everything he ever made, that nothing be lost.

The end of the matter is that there is no end. Everything that God ever gave us to enjoy he gives us to enjoy forever. I shall enjoy my train as if I were four, and Beethoven's "Appassionata" as if I were sixty-four; because, in my eternal being I shall be, I *am*, forever four and forever sixty-four.

Where does God find room for all these people and all these things? That is his problem and I cheerfully leave it with him. His ability to cope with all problems of his own making seems well established.

NOTES

1. John 14:19.
2. In chapter five.
3. Romans 13:14.
4. Colossians 1:15.
5. Walter Künneth, *The Theology of the Resurrection,* trans. James W. Leitch (St. Louis: Concordia, 1965), p. 89.
6. 2 Corinthians 4:17.

7. John Milton, *Paradise Lost*, I, 544.
8. Romans 8:21.
9. Homer, *The Iliad*, VI, 146.
10. Vergil, *Aenead*, I, 462.
11. John 6:1–14.
12. Chapter ten.
13. Acts 3:21.
14. Wisdom of Solomon 3:2.
15. "The miracles of Jesus were the ordinary works of His Father, wrought small and swift that we might take them in." George Macdonald, *Unspoken Sermons, Second Series*, "The Cause of Spiritual Stupidity."

SEVENTEEN

FRUITION

Men are immortal till their work is done.
David Livingstone

Before I first read A. E. Taylor's *The Faith of a Moralist* I knew that I was a Christian, but I only dimly sensed that I am also a Platonist, as he was. Again and again, as I read, I exclaimed to myself "But of course that's the way it is! How could it possibly be otherwise?" That first reading was in 1935. My second reading was in 1982, and it only confirmed what had been my first reaction.

That part of my passionate intuition that sees every existing person or thing as an eternal idea in the mind of God is not something that one gets directly from Plato, but it is a Platonic way of looking at one's self in particular and at realities in general. There is a fundamental spiritual affinity between the Platonic doctrine of eternal Ideas, as the perfect heavenly patterns of things upon earth, and my conviction that to exist is to be in the mind of God, and that all things are in the mind of God, and that therefore all things exist eternally.

Before I read Taylor I intuitively sensed that all true progress in life is progress toward fruition, but his suggestion that after we have reached fruition there may be progress *in* fruition has enriched my understanding beyond measure. I want to share with you Taylor's passage that I value so highly, and to do so I must quote it in full.

> The interest which sustains the good man in what he knows now as the conflict with evil of every kind need not be exhausted by the mere removal of evil; the termination of the battle in a decisive victory need not put an end to the activity to which the victory has been due, though it would make a significant difference to the form that activity would assume. To use the language of the devout imagination, the winning of heaven would not leave the pilgrim arrived at the end of his journey with nothing further to do. In heaven itself, though there would be no longer progress *towards* fruition, there might well be progress *in* fruition. Life "there" would be, as life "here" is not, living by vision, as contrasted with living by faith and hope; but might not the vision itself be capable of ever-increasing enrichmment?[1]

The fruition of a life is its completion. Why should God bring any life or any creature to completion if he does not intend to use it as a perfected instrument of his purpose? Taylor goes on to say:

> I do not see why "social service" might not be as characteristic of heaven as of earth, though it would have a rather different quality "there." On earth we have in the main to serve our neighbor by removing the sources of temptation and the other obstacles to the good life put in his way by untoward circumstances, or by the undisciplined cupidities and resentments within his own soul. Each of us has to set others forward, and to be set forward by them, in the way of purification from inordinate devotion to lower good and intensification of devotion to the highest. In the heavenly city, as conceived, for example, by Christianity, there would be no further call for this particular service, since it is a community of persons who are all in love with the highest good. But even in such a heaven, we have heard, one star differs from another in glory.[2] Even in a society where every member was in actual enjoyment of the "beatific vision," it would still remain the fact that some see more of the

infinite wealth of the vision than others, but each receives according to the measure of his capacity. We could thus understand that those whose vision is most penetrating might well have a heavenly "social service" to discharge in helping their fellows to see. . . . A friend whose vision is keener than my own may not only render me valuable help in scaling a mountain-top; when the summit has been reached, his aid may actually enable me to discern the prospect more perfectly than I should have done if I had stood on the peak alone.[3]

Any perfected human life is one in which the functions of contemplation and action, of seeing and doing, in their perfection constitute the whole being. "To give our Lord perfect hospitality, Mary and Martha most combine," St. Teresa of Avila is reported to have said. They must combine to bring us to full fruition. As long as either is stronger in us we are lopsided selves in need of radical correction. If, then, we think of heaven as the eternal family of selves in full fruition, we believe that they share not only their vision of God but they also share God's own vision of his creation and of the work that must be done to complete what remains to be completed of his creation.

I accept Taylor's vision of perfected selves in heaven, helping one another to see more and to enjoy more of the Divine Beauty; but I would add to it something that he might have rejected (though I'm not sure of this) as too materialistic. I believe that God will use each of us eternally, as he now uses us temporally, in the completion of what he has already created, and that he will also use us in the creation of worlds yet unborn—forever and ever.

We have come to believe, from our human investigations of it, that the universe is expanding. That is the scientific way of putting it. The theological way is to say that God is creating more "worlds" out of nothing, as he did this one.[4]

David Livingstone told us that men are immortal till their work is done. But will our work ever be done? C. S. Lewis observes that God "seems to do nothing of Himself that He can possibly delegate to His creatures.''[5] This seems most evident to me. God does not create us so that he can use us, but because he loves us; true. However, in his love for us he knows that the richest joy he can give us is the joy of sharing in the work and service of *L'amor che muove il sole e l'altre stelle*—"The Love that moves the sun and other stars."[6] The Love of God is the active lifeline of the universe. It is what keeps everything going. Chesterton remarked that the sun does not rise in the morning because the earth rotates in its axis around the sun; it rises because God says to it "Get up!"

At the close of chapter four I promised to give my answer to that most terrible of all terrible questions: What does God do, in the end, with the people who refuse to be his sons and daughters? To be sure, he can and does use them as his tools, whether they will it or not. But he cannot bring them to fruition, he cannot turn them from tools into servant-children, he cannot receive them into his joy, against their will. I said: "The Hebrew was a son of God in a sense that the Assyrian was not—*at least not yet.*"

Thousands of years after the Assyrian has left this earthly theater of war, how is it with him? I answer: That is entirely up to him. If he is in hell, it is because he is unwilling to receive the power to love and to learn the exercise of that power from God. Dostoevsky's Father Zossima holds that hell is the suffering of not being able to love. A person may suffer such a disability on earth. To enter heaven, either "here" or "there," one must receive this ability in full from God. If the Assyrian has received it, he no longer merely *exists* in God, in hell: he *lives* in God, in heaven. It is that choice—to love or not to love—that makes the difference, the sole difference, between heaven and hell.

In that chapter I also raised the question: "Was the Black Plague a tool of God—the God of mercy? Adolf Hitler? Josef Stalin? Cancer?" The answer to all such questions lies properly under the heading of fruition. Of anything that we experience while in time, space, and the flesh, however glorious or horrible it may be, it must be said that the end is not yet.

When we ponder human history, especially when seeking in it

whatever evidence of divine beneficent purpose there may be found therein, we often find what seem to be beneficial side effects of things that seem to be purely evil. The Black Plague, for example, was one of the causes of the breakdown in the late Middle Age of something that had to break down if the peoples of Europe were to move forward into a larger freedom of mind and life. Their progress had long been blocked by their simple trust in the omniscience of their spiritual pastors and masters in a way that was bad both for them and for their rulers. The plague came, and the prayers of the clergy did not avert the horror, and the clergy themselves died like flies along with all others. The people who survived did some hard critical thinking that proved ultimately beneficial, about whether it is wise or safe to put total trust in anybody other than God.

It is fairly easy to find evidence of such beneficial by-products of most if not all human disasters. But whether we find them or not, the end is not yet. Events, like people, must come to fruition and completion, and their end is always in eternity, never in time. Indeed, their end is always *in God.* The Black Plague ends in God, the Jewish Holocaust ends in God; Nero ends in God no less than does his sainted contemporary Paul. What that end will be for anybody or for anything, only God knows. But all that comes to pass does so, if not always by his immediate will, yet always by his ultimate will that finally determines all issues and all events. In *every* matter, the end of the matter is the triumphant fulfillment of God's will, and it cannot conceivably be a ''second best'' possible outcome for him.

The lives of rational creatures who choose to defy God's will in this life and in the next may remain in torment of nonfulfillment and incompletion forever. That must be their choice. Whether there are many, or few, or none who so choose is not revealed to us and we have no way of finding out. We shall see for ourselves soon enough.

''He who has begun a good work in you will see it through to the Day of Jesus Christ.''[7] When Paul speaks of the Day of Jesus Christ he means that final end and goal when Christ shall ''have put all enemies under his feet"[8] and has handed over to the Father a perfectly completed kingdom of love, which includes the whole creation. God may begin a good work in us while we are in the flesh. Having begun it he will finish it; we shall look upon the travail of our souls and our hands and be satisfied. We cannot be fully satisfied with anything until we see it in its end, for we cannot know even approximately what it will be like until we see it in its finished form. But we have the wonderfully sustaining promise of God that because it is he, not we, who is doing the work from its start all the way through to its end, it will be inconceivably better than anything that we ourselves might have dared to hope for.

I will close this exploration of my passionate intuition with some shining words of John Bunyan. His particular purpose in writing them was to give assurance to the sinner whose past transgressions overwhelm him and drive him to despair; but the words are quite as applicable to our hope of what we may expect from God our Home toward whom we are now journeying.

> Christ Jesus has bags of mercy that were never yet broken up or unsealed. Hence it is said he has goodness laid up; things reserved in heaven for us. And if he breaks up one of those bags, who can tell what he can do? Hence his love is said to be such as passes knowledge and that his riches are unsearchable. He has nobody knows what for nobody knows whom.[9]

Nobody knows what for nobody knows whom.
Amen.

NOTES

1. A. E. Taylor, *The Faith of a Moralist* (London: Macmillan, 1932), vol. 1, p. 408.
2. 1 Corinthians 15:41.
3. Taylor, *op. cit.,* I, p. 408.

4. If you want to say that there is only one world, one universe, I won't quarrel with you, but let's understand each other. I prefer to speak of one universe with a vast and ever-growing number of worlds in it.

5. C. S. Lewis, *The World's Last Night and Other Essays* (New York: Harcourt Brace Jovanovich, 1952), p. 9.

6. Dante Alighieri, *The Divine Comedy*, "Paradise," XXXIII, 145.

7. Philippians 1:6, a free but accurate translation.

8. 1 Corinthians 15:25.

9. John Bunyan, *The Jerusalem Sinner Saved.*

EPILOGUE

Joy, shipmate, joy!
(Pleas'd to my soul at death I cry,)
Our life is closed, our life begins,
The long, long anchorage we leave,
The ship is clear at last, she leaps!
She swiftly courses from the shore,
Joy, shipmate, joy.
Walt Whitman, *Leaves of Grass,* "Songs of Parting"

All we have willed or hoped or dreamed of good shall exist;
    Not its semblance, but itself; no beauty, nor good, nor power
Whose voice has gone forth, but each survives for the melodist
    When eternity affirms the conception of an hour.
The high that proved too high, the heroic for earth too hard,
    The passion that left the ground to lose itself in the sky,
Are music sent up to God by the lover and the bard;
    Enough that He heard it once: we shall hear it by and by.
                    Robert Browning, "Abt Vogler," stanza 11